The Dilemma of Muslim Psychologists

THE DILEMMA OF MUSLIM PSYCHOLOGISTS

MALIK BADRI

Islamic Book Trust
Kuala Lumpur

© Malik B. Badri 2016

All rights reserved. No part of this publication may be reproduced, stored in a retrieval system, or transmitted, in any form or by any means, electronic, mechanical, photocopying, recording or otherwise without the prior permission of the publisher.

First published 1979
MWH London Publishers, United Kingdom.

This revised edition 2016
Reprint 2018
Islamic Book Trust
607 Mutiara Majestic,
Jalan Othman
46000 Petaling Jaya, Selangor
www.ibtbooks.com

Islamic Book Trust is affiliated with The Other Press.

Perpustakaan Negara Malaysia   Cataloguing-in-Publication Data

Malik Babikir Badri
    The Dilemma of Muslim Psychologists / Malik B. Badri.
    Includes index
    Bibliography: p. 109
    ISBN 978-967-0526-23-2
    1. Psychology--Philosophy. 2. Islam--Psychology.
    3. Psychologists--Professional ethics. I. Title.
    150.882971

Illustrations by
Izz Al-Din Osman

Contents

Dedication... vii

About the author.. ix

Publisher's note to the first edition... xi

Reprinting the book after four decades....................................... xiii

Preface to the first edition.. xxi

CHAPTERS

1. Introduction..1
2. The Muslim psychologist as a behaviourist.............................4
3. Where psychology merges with philosophy,
   art and speculation..14
4. Islamic ideology vs. atheistic philosophical psychology.........23
5. The Muslim child psychologist in the lizard's hole................27
6. The psychometric pit...34
7. The Muslim educational psychologist who repeats
   "His Master's Voice"..42

8. The psychoanalytic abyss	48
9. The darkest depths of the Freudian pit	52
10. The dethroning of Freud in the West	57
11. As Muslim psychologists what shall we really do about Western psychology?	65
12. Psychology in the service of Islam	70
I. Psychotherapy in the service of Islam	70
II. The Islamic psychometrician	78
III. Educational psychology in the cause of Islam	80
IV. The Islamic social psychologist	84
V. An Islamic concept of personality	86
13. Are all schools of Western psychology soulless?	91
14. What about soulless schools of Western psychology?	98
15. How to help them out of the Pit?	103
I. The phase of infatuation	103
II. The phase of reconciliation	104
III. The phase of emancipation	104
References	109
Index	113

Dedication

This study is dedicated to the Muslim pioneers who broke the chains of mental slavery to Western theories and practices of the social sciences. To the father of the modern movement of the Islamization of the social sciences, Mawlana Abul A'la Maududi, to Shahid Sayyid Qutb and his brother Muhammad and to sister Maryam Jameelah. These pioneers have exposed the atheistic and Judaeo-Christian background of Western social sciences and their distorted concept of human nature. They have thus paved the way for the new generation of emancipated Islamic social scientists. The book is also dedicated to the budding group of Muslim psychologists and psychiatrists in the Muslim World, America and Europe, who are devoting their careers to lay the foundation of "Islamic psychology".

About the author

Malik Babikir Badri was born in the Sudan and obtained a B.A. (with distinction) from the American University of Beirut (Lebanon) in 1956. He followed this with an M.A. from the University of Leicester (England), and a Ph.D. from Leeds University (England). He did post-doctoral research in the Department of Psychiatry at the Middlesex Hospital, London. Dr. Badri has long experience of teaching psychology, research and psychotherapy in the American University of Beirut (Lebanon), the University of Jordan, the Islamic University of Omdurman (Sudan), and the University of Khartoum (Sudan). He has also worked at the Clinic for Nervous Disorders in Khartoum and Riyadh Central Hospital and he was the founder and Director of the Psychological Clinic of the University of Riyadh (Saudi Arabia). He is a member of many professional societies, including the Sudanese Psychological Society, the British Psychological Society, the Association of Muslim Social Scientists of the U.S. and Canada, and the British Association of Behavioural Psychotherapy.

Dr Badri has published a number of books and many papers, in both Arabic and English, including "*Islam and Psychoanalysis*" and "*Islam and Alcoholism*", both of which have been published in English.

Publisher's note to the first edition

But for lack of liturgy, psychology, with all its by-products and offshoots, has assumed in the West the status of religion, and for many people has replaced it. As in other areas of the social sciences, some Muslim thinkers and scholars have developed an amazing skill for unthinking repetition and blind copying of Western, non-Islamic ideas and practices.

'In the Lizard's Hole' is a prophetic epitaph that describes this activity very well. Some Muslim psychologists insist dogmatically on prying even into lizard's holes that have been partly or totally abandoned by their Western counterparts.

But do Muslims really need modern psychology at all? Is modern psychology wholly Western? Is there a way in which it could be reconciled with Islam? These burning questions lie lurking behind the dilemma of Muslim psychologists.

The author, a practising Muslim and experienced psychotherapist, professor of psychology for several years and an established authority in the field, takes a sombre, non-pedantic look at this dilemma, leading the way towards its solution.

He argues that the techniques which have evolved from the philosophy, basically anti-religious, underlying some of modern psychotherapeutic and psychiatric disciplines have, in fact, acquired a certain measure of autonomous neutrality, and can be useful in the service of the cause of Islam. Muslim psychologists can restore spiritual vigour to the ailing materialistic behaviourism of the West, and to Western psychology as a whole. He provides clinical evidence on how this could be achieved.

Dr. Badri's pioneering study is a warning to Muslim social scientists of the dangers of blind following of Western social theories and norms, and an effort to save Muslims from becoming trapped in lizard's holes that lie hidden in other areas of human life and thought.

Reprinting the book after four decades

I have originally planned to update this book and to rewrite it in a longer and different form. However many friends and colleagues advised me not to make any major changes to the original simplified document. One of them was distinguished professor Omar Kasule the Secretary General of IIIT who expressed this wish in an interesting way. He told me that so many scholars and students of the late seventies and early eighties have been greatly influenced and inspired by reading the *Dilemma*. I am sure, he continued, that many of them would like to see it again in its original form if only for nostalgic reasons. For these reasons, I decided that I will have the book reprinted in its original form and write my updated additions in a different book.

This small book is an extended version of a paper titled, "Muslim psychologists in the lizard's hole" that I read in 1975 in the annual conference of the Association of Islamic Social Scientists. It was published in London more than 37 years ago. In a few years, it was reprinted more than ten times and was translated to Arabic, Turkish, Bahasa Melayu, Indonesian and other languages. It was initially sold by its publishing house in London but soon other booksellers had it reprinted and sold in their bookshops and through internet services such as Amazon.com and Barnes & Noble.com. This continued until the nineties. However the need for its republication in English and other translations continue to this day. Its Arabic translation was republished in 2010 in Jordan by Depono Press. In Turkish, it was first published in 1984 by Harun Sencan. After being out of print, it was translated again by Mrs. Aynur Tutkum and republished in 2013 by Yuzaki Yayincilik.

In spite of its age, I continue to receive letters and emails from Muslim scholars and students of psychology living in various parts of the world expressing their wish to buy the book and enquiring about the address of its present-day publisher. Many of them are postgraduate students of psychology and psychiatry who were confused by the lectures of their secular professors and the readings they assigned to them. As Muslims, their hearts refused to accept such materialistic Western conceptions about human nature and its behaviour but their minds could not clearly discern their ethical and spiritual predicament nor could they come up with alternative Islamic paradigms.

I also received correspondence from practising Muslim psychologists and psychiatrists who lived for many years in Europe, America, Australia, South Africa and other Western and Westernized countries. Many were unhappy with the ineffectiveness of their Western training in helping them with their Muslim patients. After reading the *Dilemma,* they wrote to me in a warm sincere manner that at times comes close to an emotional tone that this little book has opened their eyes and helped them to fulfil the spiritual needs of their Muslim patients and clients. One of them is my dear brother and friend Dr John Sullivan; a devout Muslim from the United States. He told me in the early eighties that after reading the book, he discovered that he had all the time been in a Western 'lizard's hole' without knowing it. He decided to change his career by resigning from his Hospital work to dedicate his time to Islamic counselling. He is now a well-known author in his blessed specialization.

On the other hand, I received a few constructive criticisms of the book. In the nineties of the last century a colleague told me that he appreciated my effort at Islamization but the book overlooked mentioning the major changes brought about by the cognitive revolution. Cognitive therapy has revolutionized psychotherapy by restoring the importance of consciousness and thinking. I fully agreed with him but I informed him that the book was published in the seventies before cognitive therapy fully established its grip over classical behaviour therapy.

Though Aaron Beck came up with cognitive therapy in the 60s, it was only in the late seventies that it became fully recognized and combined with behaviour therapy to be named "cognitive behaviour therapy". When I completed my training in the Middlesex Hospital of London University's Medical School, behaviour therapy was still the sole technique of evidence-based therapy. However, as the reader will notice from the Islamic approach I used in treating the cases mentioned in this book, I was actually using cognitive therapy without knowing it.

Another positive criticism came from my dear friend

Professor Rasjid Skinner. Though Professor Skinner is a British convert to Islam, his knowledge of the religion and his depth of thought about its application by Muslim traditional psychotherapists are really admirable. He wrote his criticism in a paper titled, "Traditions, paradigms and basic concepts in Islamic psychology" that he read in the 1989 workshop on the theory and practice of Islamic psychology organised by IIIT at Birkbek College, London University.

He wrote that, "though Badri has valuably identified to Muslims the danger of swallowing wholesale the Western corpus of psychological science, he surprisingly ignores the tradition of Islamic thought among early and modern scholars and therapists". He said that my main approach in the book was to advise Muslim psychologists to "work within the empirical tradition and to distil from the Western corpus of psychology its culturally odourless, experimentally sound, objective components...rejecting the non-empirical hotch potch of myth and unproven value laden theory".

Professor Skinner's criticism is correct. Though I have clearly stated in my book that Western psychology, even in its experimental empirical approach, cannot be neutral and unbiased with respect to religious beliefs, I have intentionally stressed to Muslim psychologists to apply an objective empirically confirmed approach and to reject the non-empirical value laden culture bound Western theory and practices in their work. In doing so, I was not unaware of the valuable contributions of the tradition of Islamic thought and the contributions of early Muslim scholars and psychotherapists in laying the foundation of an Islamic psychology. In fact I have briefly referred to the work of

Reprinting the book after four decades xvii

Abu Hamid al-Ghazali when I criticised behaviourism and its atheistic approach to learning.

Professor Skinner was right in his critique but he was unaware of my real deliberate reason for this neglect. When I first read my paper in Indianapolis in 1975, Muslim psychologists in the Muslim world were still clinging to what Skinner called "the hotch potch of myth and unproven value laden theory" in psychology. In Muslim countries, Freudian psychoanalysis, as theory and therapy, had established itself as the cardinal school of psychology. Though some departments are now slowly beginning to appreciate other more efficacious therapies such as cognitive behaviour therapy, psychoanalysis still dominates the teaching of psychology in many universities in the Islamic world. This is more noticeable in Arab North African universities that are influenced by the French culture. Any criticism of Freud in these institutions is met with passionate retaliation.

My "lizard's hole" paper that I read in Indianapolis was warmly received by the audience, particularly the American psychologists who reverted to Islam. On my return to Saudi Arabia where I was professor and director of the University psychological clinic, I was asked by my friend and colleague in the Department of Psychology, Professor Abdallah al-Nafi', to translate my lecture to Arabic and to give it as a public lecture to students, faculty and interested people from the public. I did so, and as I had expected the 13 Arab faculty members of the Department of Psychology were very skeptical about my suggestions on Islamization. In the question and answer session, they reiterated the usual secular rhetoric of that time that says, "Psychology is a 'pure' science that has nothing to do with religion. You cannot talk about an Islamic chemistry or *'fasiq'* physics, so why talk about Islamic psychology?"

They were very angry at my criticism of Freud. Only one of them was fair-minded. He told me later that it was only natural for these lecturers to be annoyed. "They depended fully on psychoanalytic theory and its practices in their lectures", he said. "If you take away Freud, they would not know what to teach. In effect they were receiving their salaries from Freud!"

Accordingly, stressing the importance of traditional Islamic thought in the sixties and seventies would have obviously been untimely. My emphasis on empiricism at that time was actually a form of a gradual approach to the Islamization of psychology; a step-by-step approach to allure Muslim psychologists out of their lizard's holes. Professor Skinner's criticism came after 14 years when a large group of Muslim psychologists living in the West have already been wholly or partly emancipated.

In contrast to these friendly criticisms, there were a few secularized Muslim psychologists who strongly attacked the book and its author. As late as 1985, a Turkish psychologist bitterly attacked this book and its author in an article that I do not have now. He claimed that I was guilty of trying to revive the hegemony of religion over science and to oppose free thinking, as if Islam to him were to play the same role of the Christian Church of the Middle Ages! His article was facetiously titled "The dilemma of a Muslim psychologist", meaning that the only psychologist suffering from a dilemma is the author himself!

I hope that by now, if he were still alive, the experience of 37 years and the recent findings in cross-cultural psychology would have made him realise that no psychology can be helpful to Muslims without taking Islam as a world view into consideration. I also hope that by now he would have realised that the old battle between religion and science has already become a manageable difference of opinion.

Another psychologist reiterating more secular views was Dr Taha Amir from the Sudan. He wrote his review in a Sudanese local journal by the name of *Majalat Athaqafa Assudaniyyah*, (December, 1980, Vol. 4, 16). His main arguments were based on the early philosophical assertions of the British logical positivist philosopher A. R. Ayer who affirmed that meaningful statements are only those that can be verified by empirical certainty and not just by belief or opinion. Thus according to Ayer's early views and to Dr Amir, all religious and metaphysical assertions are *meaningless*. Consequently, the deduction of Dr Taha Amir was actually a total rejection of Islam itself and not only its use in 'contaminating' the empirically based science of psychology. I can refer Arabic speakers who wish to read my longer and detailed critique of Dr Amir's review to my article, "*Ilm annafs alhadith min mathourin Islami*". Its translation is, "Modern psychology from an Islamic perspective". The paper was published in the proceedings of the Fourth International Conference of the Institute of Islamic Thought edited by Attayib Zain Al-Abdeen in1986.

It is of interest to note that as opposed to Muslim psychologists who reject Islamization, it may be very difficult to find a Western psychologist who would argue against an Islamically oriented psychology that helps in understanding the behaviour of Muslims and finding indigenous ways to help them. It is lamentable that such

Muslim psychologists uphold these extreme secular views. In that, they are more Western than Westerners; more royal than the king.

Before concluding this prelude, I wish to thank all those who translated and distributed the book. I am particularly indebted to the late Tun Abdul Rahman Ya'kub, the former Malaysian Minister of Education and Governor of Sarawak State for purchasing a few thousand copies of the book for worldwide distribution. I must also express my thanks to those who translated the book. I am particularly indebted to Dr Mona Kintibai who translated the book to Arabic, Fadlullah Wilmot and Professor Langulung who made the Malaysian translations and Zainab Luxfiati who rendered it into Indonesian. Moreover I wish to thank all those who reviewed the book in professional journals or other references. I am particularly honoured by the reviews of Professors Afaq Ansari from Pakistan and Abdal Ali Al-Jusmani from Iraq.

Finally, my gratefulness and appreciation should go to Islamic Book Trust, Kuala Lumpur and its director Haji Koya for this new publication of the book. By concentrating its efforts on publishing Islamic books in English, Islamic Book Trust has achieved great success in promoting and internationalizing published Islamic references in a world in which the English language has become the major medium of communication. May Allah reward its executives for their blessed efforts.

Malik Badri
Kuala Lumpur, December 2015

Preface to the first edition

It is regretful that the pervasive lack of tranquillity, meaningfulness, basic human care, and spiritual purpose remain so disturbingly constant in the life of modern man. For all his seeming technological progress and advanced material knowledge, the answer to the haunting question of his own existence continue to escape him. In former times, he ached quietly, but today, behind the paper-thin facade of well-being, man is screaming. In his quiet moments with himself, what is there for him to do except ache? He has violated his own nature, which was designed to be secure in surrenderedness to Allah, the Ultimate Peace, The *Rabb* or Supreme Sustainer and Cherisher of all humanity and the Universe. Man in his confusion has taken his own inner self, which was created to be an abode of beauty, spiritual activity and light ... and filled it instead with *dunya*: The useless paraphernalia of possessions, love of wealth, reputation, and bedazzling phenomenal experience. What is the result of all this? It can be said in the misdirected masses at one level and at another level, it can be seen in the hurting human heart. Who can help? The rates of mental illness throughout the planet earth are astronomically high and frightening. Psychopathic killers, child sexual abusers, schizophrenia, mania, anxiety, and withering uncared for aged are almost household words. But still more frightening is the fact that those who are generally sought to assist the troubled hearts of men are clearly equally as sick as their patients. Sometimes they are sicker. Much in Psychiatry and Psychology is so preposterously off base, one wonders how they can be represented to any ailing person. Dr Badri has taken a bold step in presenting his reflections on what truly is a dilemma: The Muslim psychologist attempting to live a duality which ultimately is fatal. He tries to separate being professional from being Muslim in some strange way where one does not meet the other. Beyond his focus on the troubled practitioner Dr Badri has taken the whole discipline of Psychology into the examination room. His findings are quite disturbing for actually he has found that the whole Western approach to mental health is very ill. It is very apparent that Allah is out of the picture for most Western therapists. Again Dr Badri, by bringing us to see this absence is challenging the very foundations of psychology. One begins to see that any view of human nature and psychological development which does not assist the individual in understanding the interaction between himself and his creator, in the absolute sense cannot be truly therapeutic. In the absence of a true conception of this interaction and the spiritual dimension of man, the practitioner finds it a virtual impossibility to assist man in obtaining his object in individual and social life. Thus, Dr Badri in focusing on the dilemma of Muslim

Preface to the first edition

psychologists, is at the same time calling to question the range of God-unconscious Western sciences of human behaviour. As this book was presented more briefly as a paper more than three years before this publication, it has already had its time and stimulated a great deal of activity. *Alhamdulillah*, praise and thanks are for Allah, that a small nucleus of Muslim psychologists and psychiatric practitioners have already sensed the scope of Dr Badri's indictment and work is being done. The Institute Ar-Rashad for Applied Human Development and Social Research was born of these efforts and is doing pioneer work in the preparation of Islamic psychological practitioners, mental health consultation, research and Islamic applied psychological development. The book is now being represented in its expanded form. Again Dr Badri is pointing out to Muslim psychologists and psychiatrists their duty and their challenge: The conceptualization and development of a truly Islamic Psychology. The possibilities for an Islamic psycho-spiritual approach to fill the existing void in therapeutic practice are viable and exciting. Among all of those currently in the lizard's hole, the Muslim psychologists and mental health practitioners must not be trapped there. It is fine for them to visit and see what is useful, but it would be a heart breaking discouragement and a disgrace that the Muslim should die in any hole before his death. After all, Allah has shown him the favour of creating him—Man and elevating him to the high position of his khalifah and representative on earth.

Dr Muhyiddin Abd al Shakoor

CHAPTER 1

Introduction

This book is based on a paper entitled "Muslim psychologists in the lizard's hole" which I read in 1975 at the Fourth Annual Convention of the Association of Muslim Social Scientists (AMSS) of the United States and Canada. The paper was widely quoted and referred to by Muslim psychologists. It seems to have had its influence in a growing sequence of events. These were the formation of a discipline group for Islamic Psychology within the AMSS, the first symposium on Islam and Psychology in the United States, the establishment of the Institute Ar-Rashad, and the organization of the first international symposium on Psychology and Islam, held at the University of Riyadh, Saudi Arabia in the autumn of 1978.

The strange title of the "Lizard's Hole" comes from the famous hadith[1] of Prophet Muhammad (ṣ), in which he

---

1. Hadith quoted in *Sahih Muslim*, hadith no. 2002 in al-Albani's abridgement, a publication of the Kuwaiti Ministry of Islamic Affairs, n.d.

prophecised that a day would come when the Muslims would blindly copy the ways of the Christians and Jews, in spite of the obvious absurdity and un-Islamic qualities of some of these ways. This is beautifully exemplified by the Prophet's statement ... *"that even if they manage to get themselves into a lizard's hole, the Muslims will follow irrationally"*. The truth of this hadith is clearly seen in every walk of the modern life of Muslims, so much so that one hardly needs to give examples. I shall refer to this prophetic simile of the lizard's hole throughout the book.

At the academic level, in the field of the social sciences, this phenomenon of unadapted wholesale copying is most clearly illustrated. Theories and practices which are largely the product of Judaeo-Christian Western civilization have had long tenure and have dominated the social science departments of universities in Muslim countries. In addition to this, the press, radio and television have helped to establish these alien concepts among the Muslim masses.

Unthinking repetition of Western theories and practices in the discipline of psychology probably presents one of the most serious threats to the status of Islamic ideology among our Muslim scholars and laity. Western psychologists propound theories about man's personality, motivation and behaviour which are in many ways contradictory to Islam. These theories and their applications are carefully sugar-coated with the attractive cover of "science". Muslim psychologists, like their colleagues in other parts of the world, have an anxious zeal to be introduced under the prestigious umbrella of the sciences. This motivation unfortunately leads many of them to consciously or unconsciously accept blindly, and at times dogmatically, theories and practices that are, to say the least, unsuitable for application in their Muslim countries. In this book, I shall limit myself to a simplified, non-pedantic discussion about the dangers of this blind copying among Muslim psychologists and I shall try to give some concrete examples from my own experiences both as a university professor and a psychotherapist. I shall first tackle the subject in broad general terms before talking explicitly about the practices of Muslim psychologists in Muslim countries and what can be done about them. I shall give special emphasis to behaviourism and psychoanalysis since these are the main schools dominating psychology in the West and in the Muslim world.

CHAPTER 2

The Muslim psychologist as a behaviourist

A Pakistani who trains in surgery in Britain hardly needs any adaptations when he performs a surgical operation in his own country. He will find the same type of alimentary canal, the same hearts and kidneys, irrespective of belief, type of food, family upbringing or economic inflation. On the other hand, the psychology of the masses is drastically affected by cultural changes. It is true that there are very few psychological principles that have attained cross-cultural validation like the importance of reinforcement to learning, but in the application of even such a principle the type of positive or negative reinforcement used and the way it is given is largely a culture-bound phenomenon with yet individual differences within each culture.

In general, Western behaviourists and experimentally-minded psychologists are aware of the influence which culture plays in shaping the behaviour of the subjects they study. But very few of them are conscious of the role played by the ideological and attitudinal components of their own culture in colouring their perceptions and observations of these subjects.

Laboratory-minded Western psychologists, in their endeavour to be scientific, will deny that they have major beliefs or dogmas influencing their conceptualization of man. They will claim that their theories about human behaviour are based purely on empirical, unbiased observation. They will even claim to take a neutral stand with respect to the existence of God and the place of religion and to apply an objective non-biased "scientific" approach in studying spiritual phenomena. Nevertheless, they will treat man as a materialistic animal with the sole motivation for adjustment with his physical and social environment of the "here and now", which is in itself an atheistic point of view. It is a "psychology without a soul" studying a man without a soul.

In fact to be more objective, academic psychology can benefit much from accepting its subjective, unproven frame of reference and assumptions about man. A physicist can claim unbiased neutrality in observing a machine; a chemist in studying the behaviour of molecules; but no man can assume detached objectivity in studying man. Both observer and observed have their values and ossified attitudes which are shaped by environment and early up-bringing. Any degree of objectivity achieved in this social process is a product of interaction between the observer, the observed and the method of observation applied. When the psychologist is able to acknowledge his own subjective frame of reference, he will be better able to see how its influence biases his observation. Thus, if empirical evidence makes it necessary, he will be prepared to alter his position.

Many Western behaviourists may be genuinely unaware

of the influence their conceptualization of human nature can have in colouring their observations and hypotheses. Some of them may limit themselves to single-domain theories like audition, rote memory, or motor learning thus focusing their valuable researches on behaviour that occurs only under certain prescribed conditions. They generally refrain from over generalization to man's general behaviour, beliefs and values so that their personal philosophies of life have only a limited influence on their theories. But some, even among the most rigorous and laboratory-minded, seem to consciously conceal their beliefs about human nature which secretly guide their theories until, after many years, they emerge as a complete philosophy of life. A clear illustration in this respect is Skinner's *Beyond Freedom and Dignity*.[2] Skinner is one of the most influential psychologists of our time. Many acclaim him as the modern father of behaviourism. His book is a behavioural analysis, challenging many of Western man's ideals, values and concepts of human nature. Theorizing from his well-known experimental work on reinforcement and operant conditioning, he concluded that behaviours we call "right" or "wrong" are not due to any real goodness or badness in a situation nor are they due to any innate knowledge of right or wrong—*halal* or *haram*; they are simply due to contingencies involving many kinds of positive and negative reinforcers; rewards and punishments. In applying this concept to law and religion, Skinner states:

---

2. B. F. Skinner, *Beyond Freedom and Dignity*, Bantam Books, New York, 1975.

A group maintains some kind of order by punishing its members when they misbehave, but when this function is taken over by a government, punishment is assigned to specialists, to whom more powerful forms such as fines, imprisonment, or death are available. "good" and "bad" become "legal" and "illegal", and the contingencies are codified in laws specifying behaviour and contingent punishments.

A religious agency is a special form of government under which "good" and "bad" become "pious" and "sinful". Contingencies involving positive and negative reinforcement, often of the most extreme sort, are codified for example, as commandments and maintained by specialists, usually with the support of ceremonies, rituals, and stories.[3]

Thus, according to Skinner, man's religious life is reduced to nothing but conditioned responses and reflexes. Following the same line of thinking from experimental animals to complex psychospiritual human behaviour, some behaviourists even explain man's belief in God and prayer rituals which exalt Him, in such lowly terms as the superstitious behaviour of hungry pigeons, endlessly repeating specific movements which just happened to coincide with a reinforcement in a Skinner's box.

Hedonism, the theory that man's behaviour is primarily determined by the seeking of pleasant feelings and the avoidance of unpleasant stimuli is the basic foundation of all reinforcement-oriented learning theories. This

---

3. B. F. Skinner, *op. cit.*, p. 110.

hedonistic nature of man was not, of course, a modern Skinnerian discovery! It is as old as man's existence on earth. But, it must be stressed that Skinner, and before him Watson and Pavlov, have undoubtedly contributed much in subjecting classical and operant conditioning to laboratory analyses and applied behavioural practices.

However, even in their refined forms, conditioning techniques have been used by man for many centuries before these scientists were born. Skinnerian operant conditioning, in particular, was employed by ancient Arabs in training hunting dogs and falcons. The Holy Qur'an documents this clearly and considers the ability of man to condition these animals as one of the gifts of God which He taught man or which He uses to teach man.

> ... The good things are permitted you; and such hunting beasts and birds of prey, training them as hounds, and teaching them (to catch for you) as God has taught you—eat what they seize for you and pronounce the name of Allah over it ...[4]

One can still see bedouins, in remote Arabian deserts, who have certainly not heard of Skinner, 'emitting' special high-pitched sounds as conditioned reinforcers after pairing them with small bits of food given to the hungry animal. Once it learns to respond positively to these secondary reinforcements (sounds), they are carefully utilized to differentially reinforce the animal's successive approximations to the desired hunting skills. These bedouins are quite aware of man's hedonism and are

---

4. Qur'an, 5: 4.

The Muslim psychologist as a behaviourist

Ancient Arab falcon trainers. Skinnerians for thousands of years before Skinner was born.

experts in conditioning techniques, but they also possess the wisdom and spiritual acuity to see their Islamic relation to God on different dimensions.

Ancient Muslim scholars were well informed about the academic theory and some general practice of classical conditioning. Dr. Faiz Alhaj, associate professor of psychology at Mohammed Ibn Saud Islamic University in Riyadh, Saudi Arabia, has submitted his PhD thesis to a French university on the subject of Al-Ghazali's concept of the conditioned reflex.[5] Al-Ghazali was a 12th-century Muslim philosopher and theologian.

Thus a knowledge of man's hedonistic nature and its relation to various forms of laboratory and field applied researches can be dogmatically used as blinders which limit the behaviourist to a distorted tunnel-vision concept of human behaviour and the universe at large. On the other hand, such knowledge may help a Muslim scientist to see a deeper perspective in God's complex creation.

Although the Western psychological concept of human general behaviour is too limited to deal with the psycho-spiritual aspects of man, many Western psychologists also believe that the behaviouristic Stimulus—Response psychology is too restricted to explain general human behaviour. They think it oversimplifies complex human behavioural phenomena by the use of a few circular definitions and processes. For example, so many human activities are explained by Skinnerians by saying that they are reinforced. The industriousness of the hard-working

---

5. Unpublished PhD thesis, the Arabic summary of which was presented to the symposium on "Psychology and Islam" held last year (1978) in the University of Riyadh.

student is reinforced by grades and praise, the violent murderer is presumably reinforced by the thrill of murder, the stutterer by the relaxation he gets after finishing his stuttered sentence ... *etc.* Since a reinforcement is defined as that which increases the frequency of a response, we get ourselves into a tightly closed circuit of a circular definition which gives us little help in prediction. Stimulus-Response psychology is also considered too fragmentary and atomistic to give a balanced holistic picture of complex behaviour.[6]

If this is so, then the act of constricting broad psycho-spiritual religious phenomena to reinforcement contingencies and conditioned reflexes is like the blind person who tells the shape of an elephant by only feeling his tail! It is true that the elephant has a tail; it is also true that in dealing with man, religion takes his hedonism and his "conditionability" into consideration; however, this is certainly not the whole story. It is only a very minor aspect of religious phenomena in its deep spiritual dimension.

At all events, Muslim social scientists should be aware of the fact that when Western thinkers write about "religion", they generally exhibit a biased view taken from their distorted Judaeo-Christian heritage. Many of them have little or no knowledge of Islam as an ideology and a way of life. So Muslim behavioural scientists should not be apologetic about their ideology and belief.

If there is an almighty God sustaining this universe, from its tiniest electron to its greatest galaxy, and if this God sent down His Revelation through His prophets to

---

6. See for example C. S. Hall and G. Lindsey, *Theories of Personality*, Wiley, New York, 1978.

spiritually guide mankind, then the true Islamic religion cannot be viewed as an ancient Catholic Church distributing indulgence papers like reinforcement token economies; nor can Islam be reduced to an "agency" or "special government" which endeavours to control men by its "specialists" and priests, so that arbitrary concepts of "right" and "wrong" are changed to "pious" and "sinful". There is much to be said about the depth of the Islamic psychospiritual dimension and its concept of man with his hedonistic and spiritual qualities, but a detailed coverage of this subject is clearly beyond the scope of this book. However, I shall return to this topic, in a broad general way, in later sections of this study.

So when studying Western academic psychology, the Muslim psychologist should make an effort to study the philosophical background and history of behaviourism. He should also guard against the blind acceptance of allegedly experimentally based psychological theory about general human behaviour and practices and should critically examine the disguised beliefs and culture-bound assumptions behind their formulations. Armed with a strong belief in Islam and supported with scientific rigour, the Muslim psychologist can clearly see the naivete of over-generalization from birds and rats to man. Thus, he will be prepared to disqualify this transfer of oversimplified analogies from artificial limited and laboratory experiments to complex religious and psychospiritual behaviour. If he does not assume this responsibility and irrationally accepts assumptions and theories which may eventually lead him to un-Islamic constructs, then undoubtedly he will fit neatly into a "behavioural lizard's hole". On the other hand, a well-organized group of Muslim psychologists can even restore a spiritual vigour to ailing materialistic behaviourism and to Western psychology in general.

CHAPTER 3

Where psychology merges with philosophy, art and speculation

Up to this point we have discussed the position of the Muslim psychologist in relation to the simpler aspects of psychology. These aspects are more scientific in approach and pose much less of an ideological problem to Muslim social scientists, singly or at large. However, when we come to the more "fluid" aspects of psychology, we find ourselves in a state of natural confusion in which, even in highly developed Western societies no one is quite sure which lizard's hole is the one to enter into in order to solve a particular problem. This is the area of applied psychology where experts like the child and educational psychologists, the clinical and medical psychologists and the industrial and business psychologists seek to apply the methods and results of pure scientific and experimental psychology to the practical problems of man. It is the area of general theories of human behaviour, particularly in the field of personality, where theoreticians may draw from prevalent philosophies or even from theology and speculation. It is the area where the psychotherapist, faced with problems for which scientific psychology provides no ready answers, finds himself developing his abilities like an artist.

In the state of affairs which presently exists, it is not surprising to find advanced applied psychology textbooks and specialized journals full of contradictory results. Researchers tackle similar problems but somehow arguments and counter-arguments always seem to arise. Unfortunately, the researchers most often conclude in bitter disagreement with each other's conceptualizations of the same psychological phenomena. At the cross-cultural level one finds oneself unable to define vital problems clearly and precisely, let alone perform the arduous task of finding solutions for them.

For example, let us take the superficially simple general question of who is psychologically normal and who is abnormal. The field of abnormal psychology and mental health cannot yet single out specific valid norms for psychological normality versus abnormality. Three broad points of view are however generally accepted.

The pathological norm is one of these points of view. It simply considers abnormality a diseased or disordered state portrayed by the existence of certain clinically recognized symptoms. Taken to its ultimate conclusion, this point of view would consider the person who is really "normal" as the one without symptoms!

This norm could not withstand critical judgement. For one thing the symptom-free person is an ideal which does not exist in reality. Also, though psychiatrists and mental health workers may fairly agree on what theoretically constitutes symptoms, they do not do so in practice. This is particularly true in the case of less severe common emotional disorders which, nevertheless, constitute abnormal behaviour. Furthermore, the whole field of psychiatry is now being attacked by very influential opponents within its ranks. Laing and Cooper in Britain and Szasz in the USA, the proponents of what is now known as "anti-psychiatry", condemn the theory and practices of the modern discipline and its norms for diagnosing persons as abnormal. In concluding his well-known book, *The Myth of Mental Illness*, Szasz writes:

> It is customary to define psychiatry as a medical speciality concerned with the study of, diagnosis, and treatment of mental illnesses. This is a worthless and misleading definition. Mental illness is a myth.
>
> ... Mental illness is a metaphor. Minds can be "sick" only in the sense that jokes are "sick" or economies are "sick" ... Psychiatric diagnoses are stigmatizing labels, phrased to resemble medical diagnosis and applied to persons whose behaviour annoys or offends others.[7]

The statistical point of view is the second general norm. It is the graphic, mathematical approach to the question of who is normal or abnormal. The graphic concept of this statistical approach is portrayed by the curve of normal distribution in which we find most people (the normals) clustered about the middle. The fewer cases on either side of this bell-shaped curve represent the abnormals. Carried to its ultimate statistical conclusions, this point of view will consider the genius and exceptionally emotionally stable as

---

7. T. S. Szasz, *The Myth of Mental Illness*, Harper and Row, New York, 1974, pp. 262-267.

abnormal as the severely mentally sub-normal and the crippled neurotic!

From the cultural point of view the third general norm, abnormality, becomes still much more nebulous; at times it can even become a meaningless term. That is so because this point of view gives the responsibility of judging the normality or abnormality of the individual to the socio-cultural milieu in which he moves. Thus behaviour which is considered to be abnormal in one country will be quite within the norm after a few hours of air travel, or even after the passing of a few years in the same place.

I can give a few illustrations from our African and Arab culture patterns which I have already mentioned elsewhere.[8] In the un-Islamic, dying, Sudanese custom of flogging volunteers during marriage ceremonies one can still see in remote villages of the Gezira, in central Sudan, the decorated bridegroom mercilessly whipping the bare back of an enthusiastic male victim who superhumanly endures his bleeding wounds as though he is in a deep hypnotic trance. Girls reinforce this extreme show of courage on the part of the groom's friend with their usual native feminine cheers. The story is then retold in the tiny village in a way which secures the preservation of this folk culture pattern.

How does a European psychologist view this practice as an isolated form of behaviour? The Sudanese groom will not only be viewed as cruel and socially abnormal, but he would also be diagnosed as a sexual deviant who derives pleasure by inflicting pain on others, *i.e.*, a sadist. The flogged friend will be seen as a masochist who gratifies

---

8. M. Badri, Culture, tradition and psychopathology, *Sudan Medical Journal*, 10, 3, 1972.

A Sudanese marriage ceremony in a remote Gezira village. Is it chivalry or sado-masochism?

erotic sexual needs through self-punishment!

At the cross-cultural level therefore one can speak of abnormal or even pathological customs. In psychiatric units patients are treated for compulsive stealing and homosexuality. The Holy Qur'an tells about the people of Prophet Lot where homosexuality had become so strong a collective habit that heterosexuals like Lot and the faithful who followed him were openly persecuted. The Holy Qur'an brings to life the words that were exchanged between Prophet Lot and his people:

> And Lot! When he said to his people: "Do you commit the worst sin while you see (one another doing evil)?
>
> Do you approach men in your lusts rather than women? Nay, you are a people (grossly) ignorant!"
>
> But his people gave no other answer but this: They said, "Drive out the family of Lot from your city. Verily these are men who want to be clean and pure"![9]

Prophet Shu'ayb was at odds with his people because they lost all feelings of guilt with respect to the immoral act of stealing. He said to them, "*O my people! Give full measure and full weight in justice, and wrong not people in respect of their goods. And do not evil in the earth, causing corruption.*"[10] The answer to this moral command came from the chieftains of his people who said ... "*Surely we will drive thee out, O Shu'ayb and those who believe with you,*

---

9. Qur'an, 27: 54-56.

10. Qur'an, 11:85.

from our township, unless ye return to our religion ..."[11]

These verses of Qur'an make it very clear that in those societies where immoral habits have become established customs, people who exhibit high moral standards can be considered as abnormal, queer, or mentally disturbed. In fact, they may be deported or killed for being morally clean. This is stated explicitly in the Qur'anic verse,

> *"... Expel the household of Lot from your township, for they are indeed folk who would keep clean and pure."*[12]

In the light of this discussion one may well question the norms and standards for the well-adjusted normal personality upheld by modern Western psychology. Such questioning is critically important when one understands that adjustment is the main concept to which Western psychology is geared, in its theory and its practical research. Go through the criteria for the normal well-adjusted personality in any textbook on psychological adjustment, personality or abnormal psychology; you will find statements describing the well-adjusted personality as having "adequate feelings of security", "effective contact with reality", "reasonable degree of self-evaluation (insight)", "adequate satisfaction of bodily desires" ... *etc.*[13]

There is no mention at all of the other aspects of man. The religious, the spiritual or at least the transcendental.

---

11. Qur'an, 7: 88.

12. Qur'an, 27: 56.

13. See for example A. H. Maslaw and B. Mittleman, *Principles of Abnormal Psychology*, Harper, N.Y., 1951.

Likewise, there are similar conceptualizations and assumptions about the well-adjusted adolescent boy or girl, the normal child and the socially acceptable middle aged. It is clear that the criteria which Western psychology upholds for the well-adjusted individual are not developed by empirical scientific research. They are rather derived mainly from a cultural concept of modern man as viewed by contemporary Western civilisation. A concept based mainly on Western values, traditions and the powerful dictates of the modern materialistic society. In spite of their highly subjective origins, these assumptions, which may be clearly stated or taken for granted, form the milestones which give Western applied psychology its direction.

If the main aim of modern Western applied psychology is to help develop the normal well-adjusted individual along the lines of the above-mentioned criteria, then the normal Muslim, let alone the practising Muslim psychologist, should find himself in disagreement with its very foundations. Criteria which fail to include the spiritual side of man can only find anchorage in a society blinded by materialism. In such a society, the behaviour of spiritually motivated practising individuals may brand them as misfits, eccentrics or abnormals. Many practising Muslims living in the alcohol-saturated sexual revolution of modern Western societies may feel that the Qur'anic verses we already quoted about the abnormality of normals in abnormal cultures quite befitting.

Thus a true Muslim studying modern psychology in the West should find himself in disagreement with his European colleagues at least with respect to some of the issues we just discussed. More so, a practising Muslim psychologist among Western-minded psychologists should find himself positively 'abnormal', a misfit or at least untypical.

CHAPTER 4

Islamic ideology vs. atheistic philosophical psychology

When psychology blurs its boundaries with materialistic philosophical speculations and atheistic arm-chair theories, it fosters a distorted concept of man and an antagonistic attitude towards both God and religion. The best illustration for this are the psychoanalytic theories of Sigmund Freud. We shall discuss some of these theories later on in this study but it may be pertinent at this stage to give a brief statement and a few quotations condensing his views about God and religion.

In summarizing Freud's outlook to religion Henri Ellenburger writes:

> Although Freud claimed to be scornful of philosophy, he definitely expressed philosophical ideas, in the sense of materialistic, atheistic ideology. His philosophy was an extreme form of positivism, which considered religion dangerous and metaphysics superfluous ... Freud defined religion as an illusion ... a universal

neurosis, a kind of narcotic that hampers the free exercise of intelligence, and something man will have to give up.[14]

Freud developed his distorted biased view of religion as universal neurosis by comparing religious rituals and creeds with the obsessive compulsive symptoms of patients. In his book entitled *New Introductory Lectures on Psychoanalysis,* Freud says:

> Religious phenomena are to be understood only on the model of the neurotic symptoms of the individual, which are so familiar to us, as a return of long forgotten important happenings of the primeval history of the human family ...[15]

In another book he relates:

> One might venture to regard the obsessional neurosis as a pathological counterpart to the formation of a religion, to describe this neurosis as a private religious system, and religion as a universal obsessional neurosis.[16]

To Freud, the concept of God is a man-made delusion. He in fact laments that humanity still worships a false

---

14. H. F. Ellenberger, *The Discovery of the Unconscious,* Allen Lane, The Penguin Press, London, 1970, p. 525.

15. S. Freud, *New Introductory Lectures on Psychoanalysis,* Pelican, 1973.

16. S. Freud, "Obsessive acts and religious practices", *Collected Papers,* vol. II, Hogarth Ltd., London, 1950.

illusion which they created out of their childhood needs. It is the job of psychoanalysis to unmask religion and its God as it can unmask neurotic symptoms. On this subject, Stafford-Clark states:

> ... their helplessness when they have outgrown their parents ... Indeed, he commented sadly, the worship of God and the belief in an absolute system of values belonging to Him was perhaps a necessary fiction to preserve some semblance of law and order until the human race had advanced sufficiently in wisdom to do without any of the illusions to which it had hitherto clung.[17]

What should the attitude of the Muslim, any Muslim, be towards these atheistic philosophical speculations of Freud? Can a Muslim psychologist claim to be a true Muslim when he fully subscribes to Freudian theories, not only in their personality and psychotherapeutic components, but also in their ideological dimension? What is the status of psychoanalysis in modern Western psychology? What is its position among contemporary Muslim psychologists? What is the place of Freud in Arab and Muslim universities? Are there any useful aspects in Freudian psychoanalysis which a practising Muslim psychologist can benefit from, while rejecting atheistic opinions? Are there any other schools in Western psychology which give religion and man's spirituality a respectable status in their theories?

I shall not attempt to give immediate or systematically

---

17. D. Stafford-Clark, *What Freud Really Said*, Pelican Books, 1969, p. 185.

arranged answers to these and similar questions. The area of applied psychology, and psychoanalysis in particular, are too broad and complicated to deal with in the way I have tackled some problems of academic and scientific psychology. Also, I do not want to give a pedantic critical essay. So, I shall devote the rest of the book to give concrete illustrations about the practices of Muslim psychologists in various lizards' holes and to comment on the issues I just raised as they emerge in the discussion.

CHAPTER 5

The Muslim child psychologist in the lizard's hole

A Muslim professor of psychology in an Islamic country lectures to his students, advises parents on problems regarding child rearing and development and treats his patients, totally relying in all these activities on unadapted theories and practices taken straight from books published in the United States or Europe or from books slavishly translated from these sources. Isn't such a professor consciously or unconsciously moulding people's thinking, ideals and emotions so that they will eventually fit neatly into a 'Western lizard's hole'?

In talking to many Arab and Muslim child psychologists about children's problems one finds the majority of them dogmatically adhering to the Western stand of the "parents are always wrong". Somehow they have become very enthusiastic about the popular modern misconception of the "fragile personality of the child" who should be spared all sorts of physical and psychological punishment, lest he develops into an abnormal adult. In part, this may be due to the parental deprivation which many of them have received from their fathers in our traditional Muslim societies that have become harsh and un-Islamic in some of their child rearing practices.

It is interesting to note that few of them can see the inherent differences between our Muslim extended family systems and the "super-modernized" dying closed families of the West; a difference which makes the blind grafting of theories and practices of child psychology nothing less than an academic social crime. These theories of child psychology together with their experimental and practical applications are probably the principle single factor responsible for the so called "death" of the Western family. Hence, even without bringing Islam into the matter, this unadapted transplantation of American and European child-rearing practices can have its serious influence in the alienation of the younger Muslim generations. In fact, it has already started to show its effects in more modernized Muslim countries. Much more damage can be done by Muslim child psychologists if they camouflage this process of grafting by an impressive pseudo-scientific smoke-screen. This can persuade parents and teachers to stand for an operation of "unmatched transplantation" which will eventually lead to serious symptoms of "rejection".

From the Islamic point of view the preservation of extended family relations is a necessity dictated by religion (joining the ties of kinship). The popular slack attitude that "the child is always right" can only foster in the child a disrespect for his parents. This attitude, unchecked, can lead him as an adult to commit one of the most abhorrent sins in Islam, ingratitude to parents. We can further illustrate this by going back to the Muslim professor of psychology who identifies with a Western model. He tells an anxious young father of a spoiled child to be more permissive, lest the poor boy develop a neurosis. He makes the father feel guilty about having punished his son for being impolite to his mother. If the guilty father takes this "expert" advice to heart and loses the boundaries between permissiveness and over-permissiveness, what sort of an adult is his boy going to be? In fact, some scholars even in the West consider the over-permissive and undecided discipline among the modern European middle class parents, which have been directly initiated by modern psychology, to be responsible for the psychopathic and delinquent behaviour now prevalent among young people.[18] Anthony Storr, a renowned psychiatrist has this to say about the attitude of psychologists who frown upon all forms of restrictive behaviour of parents towards their children:

> ... parents sometimes find themselves criticized when their only fault is that they are parents. Parents are "good" in so far as they are protective, and "bad" in so far as they are restrictive: and since protection is impossible without restriction, no parent can escape this double appellation.[19]

I often tell my colleagues who are enthusiastic about modern child psychology, particularly those living in Western countries and modernized Islamic societies: "if

---

18. See for example J. Coleman, *Abnormal Psychology and Modern Life*, Scott Foresman & Co., 1961.

19. A. Storr, *The Integrity of Personality*, Pelican Books, 1974.

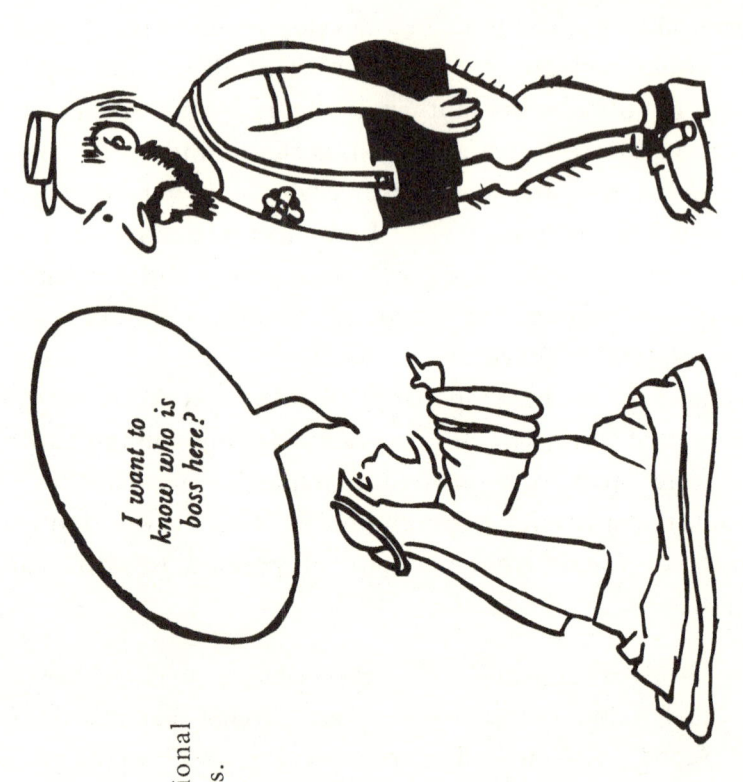

Muslim child psychologists who follow Western practices and theories like "slaves" can help to confuse the Islamic traditional roles of parent-child-relationships.

I want to know who is boss here?

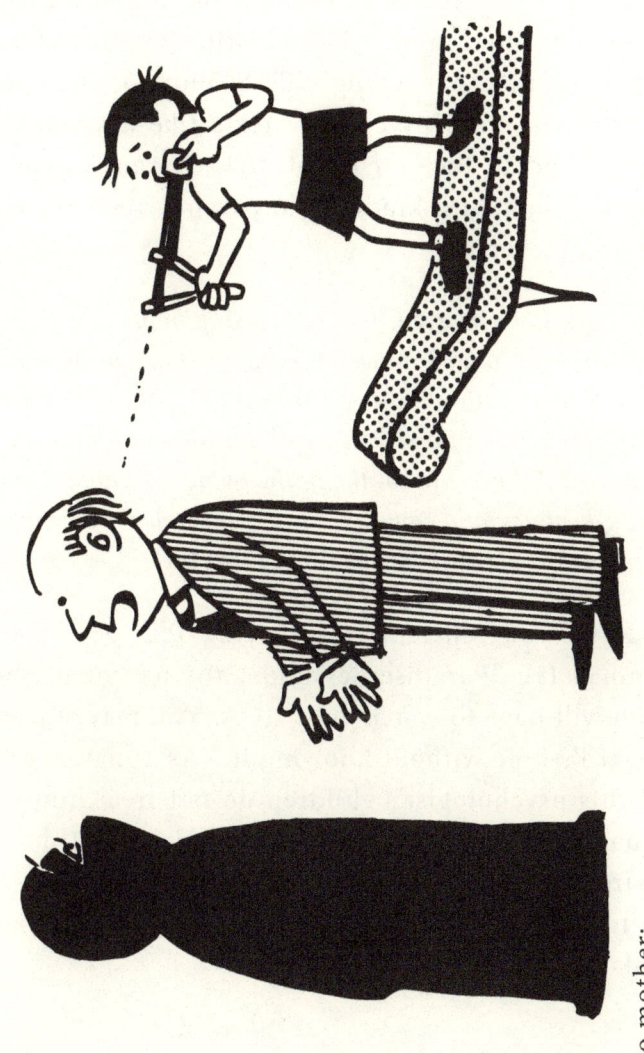

The Muslim child psychologist in the lizard's hole 31

Psychologist to mother:
If he does any of his silly behaviours just ignore him.
Behaviour which is not reinforced will automatically disappear.

you want your children to grow up as adolescents who will put their boots on a table facing your face and talk to you in the way you see in American movies; and if you want them to put you and their mother in an institution for old people when you become a nagging elderly burden, then follow your American child psychology texts like a slave. But if you still cherish the verses of the Qur'an which link worship to Allah with kindness to parents, then remember these Qur'anic verses:

> *Thy Lord hath decreed, that ye worship none save Him, and (that ye show) kindness to parents. If one of them or both of them attain old age with thee say not "fie" unto them nor repulse them, but speak unto them a gracious word. And lower unto them the wing of submission through mercy and say: My Lord! Have mercy on them both as they did care for me when I was little.*[20]

And if you cherish the saying of our Prophet Muhammad (ṣ): "Paradise lies under the feet of mothers", then you will have to watch your steps. You may slip into a large lizard's hole without knowing it." As a matter of fact, even if this psychologist's children do not treat him in the way I have just conveyed, his grandchildren will do so to their parents. Customs may take time to die but this is no excuse for one to be an active agent in the slow death of good Islamic tradition.

---

20. Qur'an, 27: 23-24.

The Muslim child psychologist in the lizard's hole

Muslim child psychologists who, uncritically, follow a Western model of child rearing can cause parents to feel guilty and children to develop an un-Islamic attitude to parenthood.

You must be more permissive, You can damage his personality

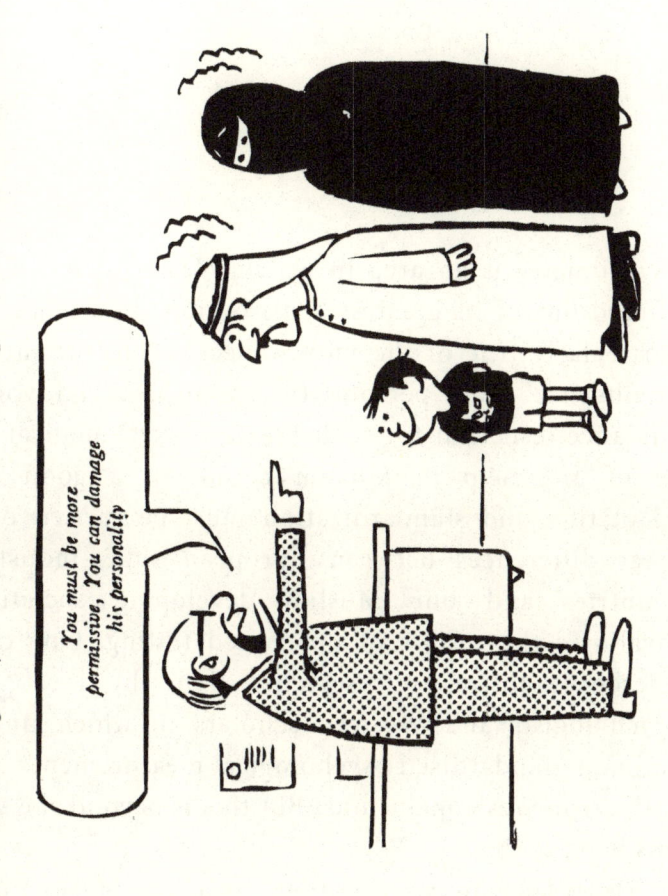

CHAPTER 6

The psychometric pit

Psychometry is an area in which Western psychology has offered one of its greatest contributions to science. This is particularly true of the more objective measurements like intelligence tests, personality inventories and vocational guidance tests. But for such Western psychological tests to be of any help in Muslim countries, a good deal of adaptation and standardization must be carried out. The great differences between European super-industrialised countries and our Muslim developing societies can invalidate the results of unadapted testing. One can give references to many researches done by local Muslim psychologists and Western scholars in which unadapted and non-standardised psychological measurements came up with erroneous conclusions. But this is beyond the scope of this book.

However, there is another group of personality tests based on vague psychoanalytic concepts and culture bound assumptions which render them unsuitable, not only as cross-cultural tools, but also as valid and reliable tests even in their native Western homeland. These are the so-called "projective techniques".

The term "projection" was originally used by Freud to describe the tendency of unconsciously attributing to other people and situations, one's own repressed feelings; generally unpleasant feelings associated with guilt, aggression and inferiority. So, according to Freud, projection is an unconscious ego defense mechanism. An illustration can be seen in the person with much repressed hostility who continuously accuses others of being aggressive towards him.

The term as used in projective techniques, is very much broadened. It is the tendency to express one's thoughts, emotions and feelings, in a conscious or unconscious manner, in structuring some comparatively unstructured material.

So the subject may be shown a set of ink-blots, black and white as well as coloured ones, and then asked to tell the psychologist what he sees in them or what they make him think of. This ink-blot technique is used in the widely known Rorschach test. Alternatively, the tested person may be shown a number of pictures and asked to write a story about the contents of each one. After each presentation, he is asked questions about the main theme of his story and its main characters. This is the method used in the well-known Thematic Apperception Test (TAT). A third popular test is the House-Tree-Person (HTP). In this technique, the subject is asked to draw a house, a tree and a person and then questioned about his drawings. A more restrictive projective test is the sentence completion, in which the subject, limited by the first part of an incomplete sentence, must produce his response of completing it.

The main hypothesis underlying these and similar tests is that in telling what an ink-blot reminds him of, or telling a story, or drawing a person, or completing a sentence, the subject will inevitably draw on his conscious and unconscious fears, hopes and emotional complexes. The trained psychologist is supposed to read back from these symbolic and concrete responses and "projections" to the subject's hypothetical complexes and hidden unconscious motives.

Unfortunately, in doing so, many psychologists "read back" from their own "projections" and psychoanalytic speculations!

As Anastasi puts it:

> ... perhaps the most disturbing implication is that the interpretation of scores (in projective techniques) is often as projective for the examiner as the test stimuli for the examinee. In other words, the final interpretation of projective test responses may reveal more about the theoretical orientation, favourite hypotheses, and personality idiosyncrasies of the examiner than it does about the examinee's personality dynamics.[21]

So the high degree of subjectivity of these tests is too obvious to dwell on. Many controlled studies[22] show that projective techniques are unreliable, giving different results on different occasions; they are vague and difficult to score;

---

21 A. Anastasi, *Psychological Testing*, Macmillan, New York, 1968, p. 578.

22 *Ibid.*

The psychometric pit

they depend much on the alleged clinical skills of the tester, which is itself a highly subjective quality; their validity is highly questionable, that is, they do not seem to measure what they claim to.

In spite of this, we find many Muslim clincians and psychometricians, in the lizard's hole, attached to projective tests and using them indiscriminately, at times without bothering to adapt them. Some of them seem to view these tests as X-rays of their subjects' minds.

For example, an Egyptian psychologist who used to work in the University of Khartoum, Sudan, gave a court testimony of not guilty, concerning a case of cold-blooded murder, based totally on his application of the Rorschach test on the criminal.

In some reputable clinics in Muslim countries, serious decisions regarding patients are at times taken on the basis of the TAT, the Rorschach or even the HTP test.

At the ideological level, the danger of relying heavily on such projective tests in training Muslim psychologists is that it may give them the false impression of psychometric "evidence" for psychoanalytic over-generalisations. Many young trainees seem to forget that projective tests are rooted in Freudian concepts and their results interpreted along psychoanalytic lines, so that the "evidence" they produce is as circular as Jiha's water wheel, as the Arabic proverb goes, takes its water from the river to pour it back into it!

Many illustrations for this circular process are seen in social psychological researches in which projective techniques are used. For example, one Arab professor (I shall not refer to his name) concluded that women in one Arab country suffer from deep inferiority and sexual "repression" because of the slowness and the quality of responses he got from them in a sentence completion projective test. His small female sample was to respond to incomplete sentences and stimulus words like "penis" and "menstruation". The natural shyness of oriental women in our Muslim countries, which slowed down the speed of their responses to sexual stimuli, was taken by this professor as evidence for sexual repression, "penis envy", and a number of other generalisations which he claimed were skilfully "uncovered" by the projective test! If another projective test was given to the same sample, and as expected, it came with similar results, it would have been taken as "evidence" for the psychoanalytic concepts of "sexual repression", "penis envy" or "Oedipus complex"! The obvious fact that it may simply be due to the great similarity between the projective techniques and to the identical methods of their interpretations by the psychoanalytically oriented testers may not even be mentioned.

Another important drawback of the better known projective techniques is that they need much time for a training psychologist to be skilful in their application. For example, the Rorschach test, which is the most widely used projective technique, is extremely complex in its scoring system. It requires considerable training, beyond that of clinical psychologist, before the person becomes a Rorschach expert. Training in the TAT may take more than quarter the time allocated for a postgraduate diploma in clinical psychology.

What will ultimately come out of this expertness for a Muslim psychologist, who will eventually work in a developing country, is a little better than wasted time. The

The psychometric pit

Doctor: What do you see in this card?
What does it make you think of?

Patient to himself: I can only see that this fellow is out of his mind!

postgraduate student of psychology should make better use of his time by training in more objective psychometrics which his people can benefit from.

In spite of all this, there is still a place in research for projective tests as patterns of unstructural stimuli, provided they are not used as material for the psychoanalytic speculations of the tester.

For example, Wayne Dennis[23], the famous American psychologist, and the author used the draw-a-man test as an index of "modernization". We asked Sudanese children in three different areas to draw a man in any way they wanted. The percentage of men drawn wearing European clothes in comparison to those in native traditional Sudanese dress closely corresponded with the degree of modernization of the city, the town and the village from which the samples were chosen.

In my book, *The Psychology of Arab Children's Drawings*, based on more than 1400 drawings, I have shown the value of human figure drawings in identifying and studying the emotional and academic problems of Arab children without going into the psychoanalytic interpretations of the HTP or the Machover's draw-a-person test. Such psychoanalytic projections were clearly found to be out of place when applied to Arab children's drawings.[24]

Even when used in this restricted manner, "culture-

---

23. M. Badri and W. Dennis, Human-figure drawings in relation to modernization in Sudan, *Journal of Psychology*, 1964, 58, pp. 421-425.

24. M. Badri, *The Psychology of Children's Drawings* (in Arabic), Al-Fatah Publication, Beirut, 1966.

bound" projective tests must be well adapted before their administration in non-European cultures. Dr. Mahmoud Azzayadi, an Egyptian clinical psychologist and the author performed a study with the TAT to illustrate this very issue. We have shown that Arab bedouins, of the Ghor Valley of Jordan, give quite different stories and themes in response to unadapted European TAT cards when compared with specially prepared identical pictures with Arab characters.[25]

---

25. Unpublished study financed by the University of Jordan, 1965.

CHAPTER 7

The Muslim educational psychologist who repeats "His Master's Voice"

Likewise, Muslim educational psychologists in the lizard's hole parrot many Western educational theories which are based on un-Islamic doctrines and practices of the contemporary materialistic society.

For example, some of them give lip service to such vague terms as "sex education" and "the true spirit of the university life". They openly advocate co-education at the secondary and university levels as the only way to teach sex education and to get rid of "sexual repression and complexes" which "psychologically cripple" our Muslim young people! They claim that segregation of the sexes in education will only make both sexes weaker in the face of temptation when they meet it and that anyway they will find ways and means of seeing each other. Hence co-education will not only breed a "brotherly" spirit between the sexes living in the sublimated "true university spirit", but also, it will reduce illegal sexual contacts between them. It is unfortunate that, because of their status, their eloquence and their misuse of scientific jargon, many lay people, even those who are religiously oriented, may take these suggestions as facts established in the "science laboratories" of the white man. Of course there are many others who will advocate these ideas for non-educational motives!

What is sex education, if I may ask, and what evidence have we for its claimed values, even in the Western world? To what extent has co-education in the West and in the modernised Muslim societies been successful in fulfilling the claims that some Muslim educators parrot? What is the concept of a well "sex educated" young man or woman in the Western world and to what extent does this concept conflict with Islam?

I have no time or space in this booklet to discuss at length the obvious answers to these questions, but it may be of interest to note that the disagreement of modern literature on the subject of sex education is probably one of the greatest in the field of educational psychology and its related disciplines. Different authors may not even agree about a specific definition to the field. As for its aims and how to pursue them, one will find himself in quick sand. One well known authority has recently said: "Two questions that have always bothered me, because I have been unable to clearly express any answers, are: 'what is the purpose of sex education'? 'what evidence and data do you have that sex education is of any value?'"[26] Another author of a well-known book writes: "More nonsense is written about sex education than about virtually any other popular subject. In

---

26. B. Fretz in, P. Fink & V. Hammett, *Sexual Function and Dysfunction*, F.A. Davis Co., Philadelphia, 1969.

spite of these writings, or perhaps in some measure because of them, American sex attitudes ... are thoroughly confused."[27]

A very crucial fact, worth mentioning in relation to this important subject, is that some Western thinkers are beginning to question the wisdom of co-education and to see the contemporary sexual revolution as a symptom and a cause for an impending doomsday of Western civilization. Among these, one of the most outspoken is George F. Gilder, whose book *Sexual Suicide* is considered an outstanding contribution in this area. It has been reprinted five times since it first appeared in 1973. Gilder was himself an enthusiast for feminist movements for many years before he came to take this stand:

> I was introduced to the subject by feminists so appealing and persuasive that it took me several enjoyable and edifying years to discover that they were wrong. In addition, my chief preparation in writing this book was immersion in feminist literature.[28]

On the subject of co-education Gilder has the following to say:

> A shift to co-education is in fact "unnatural" by most anthropological criteria. It represent a radical change in the learning environment, for both boys and girls, who mature in very different ways and phases ... And

---

27. A. Ellis, *Sex Without Guilt*, Wilshire Book Co., Hollywood, California, 1974.

28. G. Gilder, *Sexual Suicide*, Bantam Books, New York, 1975. q.v.

whatever the benefits many of the problems of America's schools — and disorders of the society—are attributable to the presumption rare in all other human societies, that boys and girls should be thrown together whenever possible.

Advocates of co-education will tell you that the boys are learning to regard the girls as "human beings" rather than as sexual objects. These are the kinds of people who imagine that most males anywhere under any circumstances — short of affliction by senility or homosexuality, never refrain from regarding females as "sexual objects". These are the "imaginative" types of people who run our schools. They tend to think that their sexual interest in budding adolescent girls is their own secret perversion. It happens to be shared by the boys in the school (as well as by all other male teachers).[29]

Gilder laments that American education took this unrepealable stand:

But there is "no turning back the clock", as they say. The few remaining sex-segregated schools dwindle in an ideological void as a species that survives the death of its philosophy and rationale. The issue today is not the desirability of co-education. Co-education is about as universal in American schools as dissatisfaction with their performance. The issue is whether the remaining male or female schools should rapidly open their doors to both sexes and whether any future institutions

---

29. *Ibid.*, pp. 219-220.

should experiment with sexual segregation.[30]

On the topic of the sexual revolution at large, Gilder speaks with unfailing bold enthusiasm and eloquence:

> It is time to declare that sex is too important a subject to leave to the myopic crowd of happy hookers, white rats, answer men, evangelical lesbians, sensuous psychiatrists, retired baseball players, pornographers, dolphins, swinging priests, displaced revolutionaries, polymorphous perverts and playboy philosophers — all bouncing around on waterbeds and typewriters and television talk shows, making "freedom" ring the cash registers of the revolution.
>
> Nothing is free, least of all sex, which is bound to our deepest sources of energy, identity and emotion. Sex can be cheapened, of course, but then, inevitably, it becomes extremely costly to the society as a whole. For sex is the life force — and cohesive impulse — of a people, and their very character will be deeply affected by how sexuality is managed, sublimated, expressed, denied, and propagated, When sex is devalued, propagandised, and deformed, as at present, the quality of our lives declines and our social fabric deteriorates.[31]

If this is the state of affairs in the West, then the sure advocative attitude of some Muslim educators and psychologists is clearly a harmful one. It can be understood if they consciously want to bring the sexual revolution of

---

30. *Ibid.*, p. 218

31. *Ibid.*, p. 1

the West to their Muslim countries and are simply using educational and psychological theory as a facade. But if they are simply echoing theories they read in Western published books then they are indeed in the lizard's hole.

A traditional class in religion. A drawing by an artist in the Institute of Education of Bakht-er-Ruda, Sudan.
(From V.L. Griffith, *Experiment in Education*, Longmans, Green & Co., London, 1953)

CHAPTER 8

The psychoanalytic abyss

A much more serious form of behaviour on the part of many Muslim psychologists is to insist on straying deep into lizard's holes that have been partly or totally abandoned by Western psychologists. In this respect, the psychoanalytic hole is probably the most dangerous and clearest example. As we have already mentioned, psychoanalysis is not simply a school of psychological treatment of psychic disorders. The universal influence of Freud has crossed the boundaries of modern medicine and clinical psychology to show its greatly felt impressions on the social sciences, philosophy, religion, art and literature. As one American historian puts it: " ... of all the ideologists influential in America, the most important, of course, was Sigmund Freud whose visit in 1909 literally caused an earthquake in public opinion".[32] The vibrations of this earthquake, with its strong rhythms, shake the very

---

32. O. Cargil as quoted by D. Bakan, *On Methods*, Jessey Inc., San Francisco, 1969, p. 130.

foundation of Islamic ideology among our young Muslim scholars.

Many Muslim psychiatrists and psychologists revere psychoanalysis and use its concepts and theories to explain all forms of normal and abnormal behaviour. This ranges from the problems of adjustment of individual patients to collective social behaviour of Muslims in various cultures. Over-generalisation from small samples and from unadapted psychoanalytically oriented projective tests is regrettably the main feature of many social psychological and social anthropological studies based on Freudian theory. When you speak to some of these psychologists, you feel as though the fluid psychoanalytic constructs like the "id", the "libido" or the "Oedipus complex" are actual measurable physical phenomena which they have seen in test tubes and not, as they really are, vague concepts that do not lend themselves to scientific verification.

In the psychotherapeutic field, psychoanalysis poses a greater problem. I was once told by a devout Muslim psychiatrist that he had told the parents of a 3-year-old child who was irritable and who always sat uneasy and scratched his anus that their child's behaviour was due to a normal phase in his sexual development since he is at the latter part of the anal stage. He is supposed, according to Freud's theory of psychosexual development, to gratify libidinal sexual instincts, by keeping or expelling faeces through the anus. Freud gives much importance to this phase and even explains adult human behaviour in terms of their childhood experiences during this anal period. Thus an adult who is greedy, obstinate and obsessed by orderliness was according to Freud an anal retentive child who used to derive pleasure by keeping his faeces in violation of parental pleading! On the other hand, anal-expulsive children, who receive much praise for defecation, may grow up to be generous and charitable adults! It was found however that that particular child was suffering from certain anal worms that caused the anal itching.

One is surprised to find such devout psychoanalytically oriented therapists among practising Muslim psychotherapists. They have read Freud carefully and have memorized some of his translated statements, yet they feel no conflict or guilt as practising Muslims. At times I feel as though these scholars have separated their emotional and mental lives into two water-tight compartments or they have succeeded in creating an apparently non-pathological form of double personalities. Otherwise, how can one explain their dogmatic enthusiasm for a person who openly ridicules religion and puts sex as the primary motivator of all human behaviour?

Much more serious suggestions and interpretations, some of them frankly sexually immoral, are given to adult patients by less religious Muslim psychotherapists and are justified to them through the influences of Freudian theory like unconscious sexual energy, unresolved complexes, repressions and similar jargon. Some of these therapists enhance the feelings of guilt in their practising Muslim patients instead of treating them. They increase their suffering by raising in them doubts about the truth of Islam in solving the problems of mankind. If Islam says do not fornicate, and the doctor, who knows the unbeatable science of Europe, says it is psychologically harmful not to, then one of them must be wrong!

The psychoanalytic abyss

CHAPTER 9

The darkest depths of the Freudian pit

A third group which pries more deeply into psychoanalytic lizard holes consists of a few qualified Muslim psychoanalysts who have almost completely "identified" with their European or American professors who have psychoanalysed them during their training. They not only use analysis in treating their patients but they also fanatically propagate its philosophical theory and ideological stand. It may be worthwhile to refer to one of these authors whose work on psychoanalysis is well known in all Arabic speaking countries.

In his introduction to Dr. Milleegi's book[33] on religious development, Professor Mustafa Zewar, the well known Egyptian analyst, says that some early attempts to arrive at a scientific understanding of the psychology of religion were made toward the end of the 19th century. However,

---

33. A. Milleegi, *Religious Development in Children and Adolescents* (in Arabic), Dar-A-Ma'arif, Cairo, 1955.

the contributions of these studies were limited. It became clear that deep research into the nature of the human psyche is necessary in order to understand religious phenomena. In other words, what is necessary is research into the area of the human unconscious dimension. Thus, according to Zewar, it was impossible for humanity to have known about the development of religion before the psychoanalytic discoveries of Freud! He goes on to expound on the Freudian speculations about the relationship between obsessional neurosis and religion which I have already quoted and to state these armchair theories as proven facts of the "science" of psychoanalysis. He explicitly says, "the psychoanalytic process fulfils all the conditions of experimental scientific research. Therefore its results are valid and reliable like all experimental works![34]

He then summarizes Freud's theory, which I have already referred to, that man's concept of God and his attachment to Him are simply a pursuit of the mirage of the father figure. The translation of Dr. Zewar's statement runs like this:

> ... There is no doubt, therefore, that psychoanalysis shows in the clearest way, the sources of religious feelings and the development of religion in man. The child idealizes his father and sees him as most powerful and knowing ... But as he passes through the well known Oedipal stage, and as he discovers his father's weakness, he finds no way but to bestow these qualities of the all knowing and powerful to a new higher being.

---

34. *Ibid.*, p. 10.

That is God.[35]

It is of interest to mention that Dr. Zewar used the Arabic word "Allah" for "God" in his actual statement.

As is known, the Oedipal stage which Freud used to explain and "discover" how man came to invent God[36] and which was parroted by a Muslim, Dr. Mustafa Zewar, is supposed to be a group of mostly unconscious ideas and feelings concerning the wish of the child to sexually possess the parent of the opposite sex and to get rid of that one who is of the same sex. This complex according to Freud is a universal one affecting all children and it emerges between the ages of three and five. The little boy loves his mother and wants her totally for himself in an infantile sexual manner but is afraid of his father's retaliation and competition. He discovers that his little sister has no penis and concludes that she must have had the same sexual urges and daddy has punished her by chopping it off leaving only a tiny protruding clitoris! The evidence that Freud produced for this theory, which gets its name and origin from Greek mythology, is from his self-analysis in which he claims to have dug out forgotten childhood memories of sexual wishes about his mother when he once saw her naked.[37] The only other evidence is "from the couch", that is, clinical evidence collected by Freud from what a handful

---

35. *Ibid.*, pp. 8-9.

36. See also Freud's theory about the origin of religion in his *Totem and Taboo*.

37. E. Johes, *The Life and Work of Sigmund Freud*, Pelican Books, London, 1964.

of his patients had told him. To this date, the only support for this postulate is of the same inadequate nature. This has led some psychologists to say that the Oedipal conflict has afflicted only one person in this world and that was Sigmund Freud himself!

Furthermore, this Freudian view about the development of religious behaviour in man, which Dr. Zewar considers as valid and reliable like all experimental sciences, is ironically borrowed by Freud from the speculations of 19th century philosophers. According to Ellenberger,[38] the writings of the philosopher Taine were developed and systematised by Tarde from whom Freud "borrowed" his views on the influence of the father figure in the development of religious behaviour in the child. Tarde believed that the child, through a process of conscious and unconscious imitation copies the father and sees him as the first lord and priest. This imitation is referred to by Tarde as the "primal phenomenon" which he first compared with hypnotism and later related to some kind of an *"invisible sexual link"*.

So it is truly heartbreaking to see Muslim scholars dogmatically accepting such unfounded theories and using them to explain to us how we come to develop religious awareness and worship Allah the Most High and Merciful. It is also disturbing to see such writings extensively circulated among Arabic speaking university students who may accept these words as coming from a high authority.

One would have expected a truly Muslim psychologist to develop an Islamic view from the very basic assumptions

---

38. H.F. Ellenberger, *op. cit.*, p. 528.

from which Freud developed his atheistic theory on religious development. For example, the inborn tendency of children to make gods out of powerful adults and mysterious forces can be viewed as scientific support for the Islamic concept of *fitra*. *Fitra* is the ethical and religious instinct, portrayed by Islam, which leads man, from early childhood, to know his true one God and to do good, and which can be distorted if the child is brought up by immoral or atheistic parents.

CHAPTER 10

The dethroning of Freud in the West

Fortunately the heavy grip of psychoanalysis on psychiatry and clinical psychology is beginning to ease in the Western world. It has been and is still under heavy fire from experimental psychologists and behaviourists on the grounds that it is based on vague concepts that are difficult to define such as "cathexis", "libido" and "id". They assert that many psychoanalytic theories are mere speculations that cannot be confirmed or disconfirmed by observation and hence are not scientific. For example how can we strictly verify that during the oral stage of psychosexual development a newly born baby gets some form of sexual pleasure from the "erogenous" zone of the mouth as he sucks? Shall we ask the neonate, "Do you get sensuous pleasure when you suck your mother's breast, son?"

Nevertheless, in spite of the nebulosity of these Freudian concepts and the theories based on them, a number of researchers were able to skilfully design empirical studies which on the whole disconfirmed psychoanalytic claims. Malinowski[39] found no evidence for the so-called Oedipal conflict among Torbiand islanders; likewise, Prothro,[40] in his valuable study on child rearing practices in the Lebanon, showed that "anal character" is not really related to toilet training in the way theorised by Freud; in a series of studies, Frankl[41] found that no relation exists between his subjects' positive or negative father images and their religious belief and attitudes towards God.

Another well founded criticism of Freud from scientific psychologists is that by basing his findings on a very small sample of his patients and using uncontrolled methods of observation he has rendered his work anything but scientifically rigorous. In spite of this, he has used these findings in extravagant over-generalisations about human behaviour, often claiming the universality of his theories. Thus, he claims the validity of conclusions drawn from a handful of Austrian female patients when applied to primitive tribes in the heart of Africa or when applied to the biographies, literary and art works of great men who died centuries before the birth of psychoanalysis. As Jehoda puts it, "The first and perhaps most frequent accusation has it that the theory [Freudian theory] is too vague to be tested, that it explains everything and therefore nothing

---

39. B. Malinowski, *Sex and Repression in Savage Society*, Harcourt, Brace & Co., New York, 1927.

40. E. T. Prothro, *Child Rearing in the Lebanon*, Harvard Middle Eastern Monograph Series, 1961.

41. V. Frankl, *Psychotherapy and Existentialism*, Clarion Book Co., 1967.

..."[42] Some psychologists believe now that Freud, who was a good student of natural sciences, was not unaware of the nature of his theory, but that he has deliberately formulated his thoughts so that they will not be tested and hence his theory becomes immune to falsification. This in itself, as philosophers of science assert, makes psychoanalysis unscientific.

Freudian theory has many loopholes that allow the analyst to claim that he is always right. Unconscious motivation in general and ego defence mechanisms in particular, are skilfully used to manipulate research data and people. Each of these is utilised in such a way as to prove the infallibility of the theory. In a simplified manner, if the analyst says that you should be having a certain feeling or that you are afflicted by one type of psychological abnormality and you agree, then he is right; if you honestly state that you do not, then it is in your unconscious. Reaction formation, an ego defence mechanism, will make you deny consciously what you really are unconsciously!

Researchers in the history of psychology and psychoanalysis have also unearthed important pertinent documents from the biography of Freud's associates, from his letters to them and from other historical studies in the field. Of these, the most important is perhaps Ellenberger's monumental book, *The Discovery of the Unconscious*.[43] Until recently, even Freud's most severe critics have at least credited him with originality. But these studies have shown

---

42. M. Jehoda, Social Psychology and Psychoanalysis: A mutual challenge, *Bulletin of British Psychological Society*, 25, 89, 1972.

43. H. F. Ellenberger, *op. cit.*

beyond doubt that many of his ideas and even his terminology should be credited to others. Most of the ideas that Freud borrowed from others were the more valuable in his theory and were those that would have stirred no ill feelings toward psychoanalysis. It is probably this that have led Eysenck to say about psychoanalysis: "what is true in these theories is not new and what is new is not true"![44]

We have come to know now that many of these new aspects in Freudian theory were in fact drawn from traditional 'Jewish lizards' holes'.

Of interest in this respect is Bakan's valuable study. He shows that Freud deliberately used his early Jewish Talmudic training as his major source of psychological data and not his patients as he contended.[45] A more recent book in this area is Marthe Robert's *From Oedipus to Moses*, for which she was awarded the French Gulliver Prize. In this study, she unveiled the strong influence of Freud's Jewish background in the genesis of his psychoanalytic theory, documenting her work mainly from Freud's own autobiographical data and correspondence. On the subject of Freud's "Jewish spirit" Marthe Robert has this to say:

> The intimate relationship between psychoanalysis and the "Jewish spirit" is so obvious that few of those who refer to it stop to define the "Jewish spirit" or to ask how it has been transmitted from generation to generation.

---

44. H. J. Eysenck, Experimental study of Freudian Concepts, *Bulletin of the Br. Psych. Soc.*, 25, 89, 1972.

45. D. Bakan, *Sigmund Freud and the Jewish Mystical Tradition*, Van Nostrand Co, Princeton, 1958.

Though he does not dwell on the subject (Jewish spirit) Freud often speaks of it, especially in his letters and in his autobiographical study. Indeed, he was the first to relate his discoveries to intellectual and moral traits which, he believed, derive from his origins. Thus in his address to the B'nai B'rith—a Jewish liberal organization in which he was active for twenty years and to which he belonged up to the time of his death— he attributes the two qualities that he regards as decisive for the development of his work essentially to his "Jewish nature". Because I was a Jew I found myself free from many prejudices which restricted others in the use of their intellect and as a Jew I was prepared to join the opposition and to do without agreement with the 'compact majority'. Not only does Freud speak of a "Jewish nature," specially equipped to take its place in the forefront of intellectual struggle; he also draws the radical conclusion that psychoanalysis could be invented only by a Jew and that this explains why despite its urgency this investigation of the human psyche was so long delayed. Why, he asked Paster Pfister in the course of a friendly argument, didn't one of those pious men create psychoanalysis? Why did it have to wait for an absolutely irreligious Jew?[46]

This fact about the Jewish influence on the development of psychoanalysis is of great pertinence to our discussion of the lizard's hole as described by Prophet Muhammad (ṣ).

However, the greatest blow to psychoanalysis has come ironically from the field of psychological therapy. This is

---

46. M. Robert, *From Oedipus to Moses*, Routledge and Kegan Paul, London, 1977, pp. 3-5.

the area where Freud had always felt most secure and had used his alleged successes in it as a justification for the application of his theory even in spheres totally unrelated to therapy such as religion and philosophy. In his article entitled "Neurosis of demoniacal possession", Freud writes:

> We hear once more the familiar criticism of psychoanalysis that it regards the simplest affairs in an unduly subtle and complicated way, discovers secrets and problems where none exists, and that it magnifies the most insignificant trifles to support far reaching bizarre conclusions...[47]

To defend these sound familiar criticisms Freud found no better support than the claimed success of his theory in understanding and treating neuroses. He goes on to state in the same article:

My justification for so doing lies in the success of our investigations into the nature of the neuroses in general. Speaking in all modesty, we may venture to say that even the most obtuse amongst our colleagues and contemporaries are beginning to realize that no understanding of neurotic states is to be attained without the help of psychoanalysis.

"With these shafts alone can Troy be taken", as Odysseus admits in Philoctets of Sophocles.[48]

It seems now from a number of controlled researches on the real efficacy of psychoanalysis as a psychological

---

47. S. Freud, *Collected Papers*, Vol. IV, Hogarth Press, London, 1950, pp. 447-448.

48. *Ibid.*, p. 448.

therapy that Troy has not been taken, at least not in the way in which Freud "modestly" asserted. Controlled studies in which a group of neurotic patients received psychoanalysis and psychoanalytically oriented psychotherapy in hospitals, while a carefully matched control group received no therapy at all, for lack of hospital beds or other reasons, were compared after a period of one to two years. The startling result was that an equal proportion of patients improved in each group. The experiment was repeated with soldiers who had suffered a neurotic breakdown, with children suffering from emotional disorders and with delinquents. The result has always been the same. No difference of any statistical significance.[49] The impact of these researches as well as the rise of new schools of psychological therapy which are much more effective in treatment and which offer alternative simpler and more parsimonious scientific explanations for psychological disorder, such as behaviour therapy, were among the main reasons for the dethroning of psychoanalysis. Thus while we see today many psychologists, particularly in Britain and Europe, turning away from psychoanalysis, and while we see the rise of new competitive schools that are comparatively not in conflict with Islam, we still see many psychologists in Muslim countries securing themselves in Freudian lizard's holes. Some of them, like Dr. Zewar, allow themselves to explain the most noble of human feelings, the relation between children and parents, and the greatest gift that Allah has given to Muslims, their faith in Him, in terms of Oedipus complexes and little boys afraid to have their penises cut off by their fathers.

---

49. R. S. Rachman, *The Effects of Psychotherapy*, Pergamon Press, 1971.

I hope I have made my point that some Muslim psychologists insist dogmatically on prying in lizard's holes that have been partly or totally abandoned by Western psychologists. It is saddening to find that many of them continue to parrot such Western psychological theory and to follow their practises with this uncritical allegiance. This mental enslavement, as we have seen, is unfortunately not limited to scientific psychology. Many devout followers of anti-Islamic philosophically orientated Western schools of psychology helped these schools to flourish in many Muslim university departments of Psychology, inspite of their diminishing influence in their mother Western countries.

CHAPTER 11

As Muslim psychologists what shall we really do about Western psychology?

Now that I have discussed some of the actual and potential threats of modern Western psychology in relation to Islamic ideology, and after citing examples about the unadapted parrotry of the practices of Muslims dedicating themselves to a Western model of "psychologist" or "psychoanalyst", I feel obliged not to put down my pen before giving my tentative answers to two difficult questions. The first is, what is the position of the very few Muslim psychologists who are out of the lizard's hole toward modern Western psychology? The second, what can they do about the overwhelming majority of their colleagues who have committed themselves to Western psychology?

A Saudi educator once said after a very illuminating public lecture-discussion delivered by Professor Muhammad Qutb, the well known Egyptian Muslim thinker, that we, as Muslims, do not need modern psychology: This subject, he said, with all its branches, is a constellation of theories and practises which are the alien product of a *kafir* Western civilization. He strongly urged that it should be deleted from the curricula of teacher-training colleges in Saudi Arabia until such a time may come when Muslim scholars write up new psychology texts based on Islamic ideology. Recently, one Muslim university has actually closed down a division of its psychology department because of unIslamic psychological material strongly propagated by a certain professor.

In answer to my first question, should the practising Muslim psychologist take such a stand? If he does so, I believe, he will be throwing out the bath water along with a number of healthy babies; valuable gems with much trash.

For one thing modern psychology is not all "Western". It is largely the accumulated experiences of men about men. Modern psychology has subjected some of these experiences to more refined ways of observation, experimentation and measurement. One will find ideas dating back to Aristotle and other Greek philosophers even in such branches as modern learning theory. In fields like personality, social psychology and even psychotherapy we will find much of what Eastern thinkers have contributed through the ages even though they may not be credited for all they have done. Among these we will find a number of our own Muslim ancestors like Ibn Sina in psychotherapy and psychiatry, Ibn Khaldun in sociology and social psychology, Ibn Sirin in dream interpretation and al-Ghazali and al-Muhasibi in personality studies. Thus some of the babies who may be wrongly thrown away with the water may be our own blood relatives. We should also not forget to mention that, even today, some of our eminent Muslim psychologists made great contributions to Western academic and applied psychology. Clear examples are found in the work of Abdul Azeez al-Kousi in the factorial analysis of intelligence, Sherif in the field of experimental social psychology and Mustafa Suef in personality and in addition.

Furthermore, modern scientific psychology, though a child of Western civilization, has developed many useful tools and practices which no nation can do completely without if it intends to technologize and develop its educational, military, and medical systems.

As already mentioned, intelligence tests are considered a great breakthrough in the measurement of human abilities. Their value in education, industry and other fields cannot be denied. They were used with great profit during peace and war. Other types of tests measure manual dexterity, attitudes, vocational orientations, emotional disturbance and other variables. Even some special equipment was devised to detect emotional changes in man which are successfully used in lie detection, psychotherapy and for other purposes.

Muslim countries also need the contributions of psychology in the field of learning. This is one area which lends itself to pure experimental research and one in which there is little room for speculative nonreligious theories. Excellent researches have been performed with animals and human beings to answer such questions as the nature of learning, motivation and reinforcement, transfer of training from one field to another, the nature of remembering and the reasons for forgetting and similar topics. Learning theorists and experimentalists have helped to revolutionize schools. With the help of other educational psychologists they have succeeded greatly in setting the accent on better methods of teaching. They have also developed much helpful equipment and materials. These are things such as teaching machines that use programmed instruction, audio-visual aids such as motion pictures, models and television as well as other direct experiences which help the child to learn by doing. Muslim nations can make much use of these contributions without being affected by their philosophical background. One feels depressed when seeing our traditional schools and archaic teaching methods which succeed only in developing non-critical thinkers and good memorisers among our rising Muslim generations. To make full use of this aspect of psychology it will of course be necessary for our Muslim educational psychologists to help develop their own tools and methods of application of the theories and principles that have proved their worth in the West. Again I must say that this is the job of an association of Muslim psychologists co-operating with a number of psychology departments in Islamic countries.

The disciplines of psychotherapy and psychiatry have also developed efficient techniques for dealing with psychological sufferings. Though, as we have seen, the philosophy underlying some of these methods may be an anti-religious one, at least in a disguised implied manner, the very useful techniques that have evolved from them have acquired some sort of autonomous neutrality.

As has been mentioned earlier, behaviour therapy and behavioural psychotherapy, which are founded on learning theory and experimental psychology, have proved themselves by the help of controlled experimentation, to be very efficacious therapies for some neurotic disorders like phobic and obsessional reactions and sexual dysfunction. The behaviour therapist works like a technician attacking the symptoms themselves without necessarily going into unconscious or sexual interpretations as psychoanalysists do. He considers the neurosis as mainly a learned habit and helps the patient to unlearn it and to learn new adaptive habits in its place. In its theory and its practice, behaviour therapy is mainly a process of learning and unlearning by conditioning and deconditioning and cognition. It will be a pity if these methods are not made use of in any Muslim country under the guise of "don't need any Western *kafir* psychology in our Muslim society".

CHAPTER 12

Psychology in the service of Islam

In fact, the practising Muslim psychologist can go out of his way to use these therapeutic, as well as any other useful psychological, techniques for the cause of Islam.

In this section, I shall give a fairly detailed account about some of the useful activities which a Muslim psychologist can carry out in order to put his professional training, with its existing limitations, in the service of Islam and the welfare of Muslims. I shall start with the Muslim psychotherapist.

i. Psychotherapy in the service of Islam

Unlike psychologists in the lizard's hole, the dedicated Muslim does not see his patient or the process of psychotherapy through the tunnel vision of the school of therapy in which he received his training. He realizes that the person coming for help is a Muslim with special unique problems coloured by the specific culture in which he lives.

To illustrate what I mean, I shall relate some of my experiences in behaviour therapy which I have already referred to in an earlier publication. I have always found my patients' belief in Islam a very useful help in their treatment. A young female Moroccan patient was referred to me in 1965 in the neuropsychiatric section of the University of Rabat's Teaching Hospital. She had a number of complaints, among them generalised anxiety, feelings of inadequacy and depression and some phobic reactions. Her case and the then new technique of desensitisation the author used in her treatment are described in detail elsewhere,[50] but what concerns us here is that she was admitted to the hospital twice for a period of almost a year between which she had been taken to a harsh native healer. She could get no help from traditional nor modern individual and group psychotherapy, nor from tranquilizing drugs. In one of the group sessions, I was reading a passage from the Qur'an on the forgiveness of sinful behaviour as a moral support to a male patient who was leaving hospital:

> And vie with one another for forgiveness from your Lord, and for Paradise as wide as are the heavens and the earth, prepared for those who ward off (evil). Those who spend (of what Allah hath given them) in ease and in adversity, those who control their wrath and are forgiving toward mankind; Allah loveth the good. And those who, when they do an evil thing (Fahisha) or wrong themselves, remember Allah and implore forgiveness for their sins—who forgiveth sins save Allah

---

50. M. Badri, A new technique for the systematic desensitization of pervasive anxiety and phobic reactions, *Journal of Psychology*, 65, 201-208.

only?—and will not knowingly repeat (the wrong they did).[51]

To this she responded with unexpected tearful emotion. I was then asked by the chief psychotherapist, Dr. H. Habib, to take her up for treatment. I continued to read to her Qur'anic passages which deal with the subject of Allah's forgiveness of all sins and to explain all that in simple language. That was the beginning of an emotional confession and a very quick improvement through the application of behavioural therapeutic techniques.

Dr. Habib's comment to me after this successful dramatic improvement was: "I have always kept a copy of the Holy Qur'an in my office in the hospital for the last three years. It never occurred to me at any time to bring it down from the book shelf as a therapeutic aid to any of my patients".

Another Sudanese female patient presented herself with the common obsessional neurosis of hoarding waste paper and of the long and tiring repetition of prayers. As is known, the practising Muslim should offer prayers five times every day which takes about 5 to 10 minutes per prayer; but this miserable patient had to spend hours every day. Whenever she was about to finish one prayer she doubted whether she had carried out her rituals correctly and so she cancelled it and started from the beginning. Often she repeated this process until physically she became very tired. She said that she did not mind the hoarding symptom but she wanted very much to rid herself of her own self-instated trouble in carrying out rituals. In fact,

---

51. Qur'an, 3: 133-135.

when I first saw her she was performing her own invented ritualistic behaviour in an unsuccessful attempt to insure correct prayers.

It may be worthwhile in this connection to make a passing remark about those who believe in the Freudian concept of religion as the universal obsessional neurosis of mankind. Such people fail to see that man has ritualised all aspects of his social life. Religious rituals are not the only ritualised activity of man. More seriously, and I am addressing myself to the Muslim psychologists, they have failed to see the obvious difference between those who enjoy religious rites like prayer, to the extent of losing themselves in transcendental ecstasy, and the real obsessionals, like our patient here, who may come to dislike prayer but are unable to stop themselves from the repetitions of its rituals. It is really unfair and unscientific to put these categories into one basket of universal obsessionalism.

In introducing his famous book, *The Individual and his Religion*, Gordon Allport, the well known American psychologist, has this to say about the spiritually colour blind, biased theoreticians who fail to differentiate between the "psychology" and the "psychopathology" of religion.

> ... I am seeking to trace the full course of religious development in the normally mature and productive personality. I am dealing with the psychology, not with the psychopathology of religion. The neurotic function of religious belief ... is indeed commonly encountered, so commonly that opponents of religion see only this function and declare it to dominate any life that harbours a religious sentiment. With this view I

disagree. Many personalities attain a religious view of life without suffering arrested development and without self-deception. Indeed, it is by virtue of their religious outlook upon life — expanding as experience expands—that they are able to build and maintain a mature and well-integrated edifice of personality. The conclusions they reach and the sentiments they hold are various, as unique as is personality itself.[52]

We return now to our prayer obsessional patient. She was first seen by a Sudanese psychoanalytically oriented psychologist who had tried his art without success. The psychiatrist who referred her had tried all sorts of drugs, E.C.T. and electro-sleep therapy without improvement to the obsessional rituals. I first tried classical behaviour therapy; aversion and later systematic desensitisation therapies with disappointing results. I knew then that obsessional neurosis is a difficult disorder to treat and that one of the most successful behavioural techniques with it is to prevent the patient from doing his rituals in spite of the intense anxiety he will at first develop during the treatment, e.g. to "imprison" the patient with obsessional hand-washing in a room where no running water is available. But can I prevent my patient from prayers? This can neither be accepted by me, the patient, her family nor the community at large.

By explaining to her the Islamic rules for prayer she found that when she prays behind an imam, who leads the prayer, she will shoulder no responsibility for the prayer.

---

52. G. Allport, *The Individual and his Religion*, Macmillan, New York, 1953, p. viii.

Psychology in the service of Islam

She just follows the movements of the prayer after the imam and simply listens to passages from the Qur'an if the prayer is done loudly. These rules were explained to her in detail and she was asked to check them with learned Muslim sheikhs. She was then told not to say any prayer alone. There is no priesthood in Islam and anybody can act as her imam in prayer. Luckily for her we were then nearing the month of Ramadhan during which interested Sudanese older woman attend the long voluntary evening *tarawih* prayers in mosques. I told her to attend one mosque in Omdurman where the imam chants their Qur'an—during prayers in a beautiful, moving way: I said my prayers in the same mosque and she came every evening with her mother to follow the complete prayer which takes more than an hour to finish, after which we occasionally had short interviews. At the end of the month of Ramadhan the prayer obsessional ritual had completely disappeared while the untreated hoarding symptom remained intact.

I have also used the same "modelling" technique in helping a young Saudi male patient get over his obsessive compulsive rituals with respect to ablution (*wudu'*).

When it comes to evoking religious emotion to help the neurotic and insecure patient achieve relaxation and transcendental tranquillity, Islam can offer an overflowing spring of sentiments. As an illustration, a male 35-year-old patient was referred to me, in 1970, in the Clinic for Nervous Disorders, Khartoum, North Sudan, presenting with a crippling phobia of death and severe hypochondriasis. His neurosis failed to respond to traditional psychiatric treatment with drugs and supportive therapy. His troubles started a few months after the sudden death of his mother. He was her favourite son. During his grief, he saw a vivid dream in which his mother had told him that his uncle, then a man of forty, would soon join her and then his turn would be next. He took the dream lightly until, after a few months, this uncle died in an accident. On hearing the tragic news, his phobic reaction took a sudden, almost overwhelming, turn.

When I saw him, his condition had deteriorated to the extent that his work and family life had already been adversely affected. He had spent much of his savings on "being treated" for imagined physical disorders and his life had been continuously haunted with impending death and catastrophe.

Though I used classical systematic desensitisation therapy, in which his mother's dream and other death scenes were imagined and desensitised, Islamic sentiments and concepts about the real value of life, of death, and of life after death were strongly evoked and discussed whenever appropriate. These sentiments and cognitive experiences were at times related during fearful scene presentations. In between imagined death related scenes, the patient deeply relaxed his body and listened in tranquillity to a highly sentimental narrative about the life of Prophet Muhammad (ṣ), with emphasis on his attitude to life. I remember vividly being myself moved by seeing tears streaming from the trembling closed eyelids of my spiritually motivated patient.

Gradually he was able to return to his normal pre-morbid self, and even to attend funeral ceremonies and mass prayers for the dead, an activity which he had totally avoided during his illness.

In the area of psychotherapy and counselling, I can give a number of personal experiences in which patients do not only improve after therapy, but they also become better Muslims. I strongly believe that the Muslim psychologist should discard the Western model of a detached, morally neutral, empathic therapist. The non-directive Rogerian counsellor is at peace with the Western democratic belief in the private liberty of the individual to constructively shape his life or morally corrupt it in the way he pleases. He can be an alcoholic or a homosexual and is accepted as such, provided he does not infringe on other people's rights. To take this attitude to its extreme will be un-Islamic. If he feels his direct intervention may help to guide the unhappy "sinful" patient back to psychospiritual mental health, then the Muslim counsellor should do so, but in a *warm, sympathetic manner.*

For example, in treating a Pakistani doctor whose suicidal reactive depressive problems were associated with a highly authoritative father, I had to help both father and son to see the duties and rights which Islam sets to guide this noble parental relationship. In so doing, I had to visit the father for private interviews and later to hold long discussions with both. The outcome of the therapy was rewarding, *Alhamdulillah,* to all of us.

One is happy to hear that since the publication of this book in article form, more than three years ago, Muslim psychologists Muhyyi Abdul Shakoor, Rasheed Hamid and Attya Swellim have started working on the development of a new Islamically oriented psychospiritual therapy which will be in print soon.

We have thus far been discussing what a practising Muslim psychotherapist can do in employing the useful areas of modern psychology for the cause of Islam and

Muslims. Now, what can a Muslim psychometrician do in this area?

ii. *The Islamic psychometrician*

We have already discussed some of the unacceptable practices of Muslim psychometricians in the lizard's hole. Outside the hole, a number of non-European psychologists, Muslims and non-Muslims, carried out monumental researches to adapt and standardise many useful objective Western psychological tests. More often than not, Muslim psychologists will find that further tailoring and standardisations are needed for different sub-cultures in the same Muslim country. The use of such refined measurements in schools, hospitals, industry and the military is a great service which a Muslim psychologist can present to his nation. It is a service to Muslims and hence it is for the cause of Islam.

However it is important for Muslim psychologists not to rely solely on the adaptations of existing measurement tools. They must develop the originality and the self-confidence which will allow them to use the methods and principles of assessment to create their own measurement tools. They can even tap the measurement of new variables peculiar to Muslim subjects, thus offering their own contributions to psychology and breaking the chain of mental slavery to the West. Though there are rare cases of Muslim scholars who have already started in this line, for example Egyptian psychiatrist Mohammad Yousif Khalil, who is working on a test for a religious Islamic norm, this task is not really the job of a few individuals. It must be the work of a society of Muslim psychologists whose members can compare notes and coordinate their efforts to carry out this arduous task.[53]

One can predict that such novel tests may, one day, be of special value in hitherto untapped areas of special importance in the renaissance of the Islamic way of life and its propagation. One such vital field is that of modern Islamic movements; the organised educated Muslim youth who shoulder the formidable responsibility of socially, spiritually, and politically reinstating Islam, in its true dynamism and comprehensiveness, to its rightful position of authority. Unfortunately, the crude methods now used in the selection and training of young men and women, who actually carry out most of the work of directing these Islamic revolutionary groups, have subjected these movements to serious conflicts from within its ranks as well as more dangerous clashes with local governments. It may be argued that many troubles which these Muslim movements continue to face are caused by external political and social powers antagonistic to Islam, and are hence unavoidable. However, a critical and unbiased study of the recent history of such conflicts, for example in Egypt, Syria, Pakistan, and the Sudan, will clearly reveal this lag in the selection and training of Muslim workers. One emotionally disturbed ringleader or hypomanic member can overreact aggressively towards the dictatorial president of his country to lead the whole group of hundreds of thousands of pious innocent young people to prisons and harassment.

One feels sure that adapted Western psychometric experiences supported with the original contributions of

---

53. One is happy to see that a Society for Muslim Psychologists has already been organised in the USA.

devoted Muslim psychologists and other social scientists will improve much in the selection, training and organisation of these great movements and will help to, at least, reduce avoidable conflicts.

iii. *Educational psychology in the cause of Islam*

Another area where devoted Muslim psychologists can put their academic training in the service of Islam is that of educational psychology in its broad perspective. The field which cries for immediate help is ironically that of Islamic education among Muslims. The teaching of Islam, as a school subject, in all the length and breadth of our Muslim world is in a very poor condition indeed. It is really astonishing that Islam continues to gain ground as a political and social force in Muslim countries in spite of the disheartening manner in which it is presented to our primary and secondary school children, who on top of that, are being subjected to the influences of Western and Eastern anti-Islamic cultures. For this reason, I should like to discuss this subject at some length.

In Muslim countries which suffered from long years of imperialist Western domination, open anti-Islamic military aggression and long-range educational and socio-political plans have succeeded in alienating sincere Muslim workers and in demoting Islamic education to a much inferior position in comparison to modern Western schools set up and protected by these imperialists. This duality of "religious" and "secular" educational systems created a serious schism in which the sophisticated highly paid Western educated Muslims looked down upon the graduates of the traditional poorly salaried religious schools.

Either because of these imperialistic influences, or out of sheer decadence, the typical picture of the teacher of "Islamic religion" in many Muslim countries has become that of a highly traditional, rigid, bearded sheikh or mullah. He does not speak a European language, is not schooled in attractive "secular" subjects like science, geography and mathematics, and is generally an unsophisticated and uncultured person in terms of modern standards. In some Muslim countries many teachers of religion are either very old or blind.

The method of instruction the teacher knows best and uses most is the archaic "verbalism" trio of dictation, memorisation and regurgitation. Whether or not they really understand the religious material presented, the most important issue which the teacher stresses, is the ability of children to memorise what he dictates. At times this memorisation is about the only activity young children can do since the material taught is high above their ability to conceptualise. That is so because, as a result of the imposed schism of secular and religious systems, and/or, because teachers know little outside their traditional grounds, the curriculum of Islamic studies taught in modern schools is mainly limited to religious rites, elementary jurisprudence (*fiqh*) and the memorisation of some parts of the Holy Qur'an and the Prophet's hadith. Thus Islam as a comprehensive and revolutionary way of life is reduced to a non-dynamic small area far from the warm interaction of modern life.

To make things worse, most teachers use negative practices of severe physical punishment, reproof, and the deductions of grades in order to ensure that children take their memorisation assignments seriously.

This distressing situation will have to change. At the university level, some Muslim universities, like the Islamic University of Omdurman, Sudan, and Al-Azhar University of Cairo, have already taken preliminary steps to present Islamic studies in a more comprehensive and modernised approach. However, the teaching of Islamic studies at the primary and secondary levels still remains to be drastically reviewed. Thus, the sincere Muslim psychologist should have a major role to play in this holy *jihad* of changing the face of Islamic education.

Islam is not simply a "religion" in the narrow Western meaning of the term. It is an all-embracing style of life. The Holy Qur'an directs Muslims in matters as private as their sexual relation with their spouses, and as broad and public as the way a Muslim state should run its economic system. It preaches spiritual guidance in relation to every subject under the sun; human embryology, astronomy, geology, law, social change, nutrition *etc*. Thus, in fact, in a real Muslim state, the teaching of Islam should ideally be fully integrated with all subjects of the school curricula; each teacher tackling certain areas of Islamic studies within the integrated curriculum of his subject area.

If this ideal integrated curriculum cannot be developed now, Islamic studies, as a separate school subject, should at least reflect this broad and interactional property of Islam. The curriculum should include living issues which children face at different stages of their lives. In this connection, the expert advice of Muslim developmental and child psychologists is certainly crucial. For example, I should imagine that the subject of sex education, from the biological, moral and Islamic aspects, would be included at different phases of the curriculum.

As for the qualified instructors and the teaching methods of this broad curriculum, something must be done about the majority of existing traditional teachers. Most of them are sincere Muslims, but their ability to present Islam to children in this universal perspective is very much doubtful. Honestly, I can only see one very valuable contribution which these traditional teachers can continue to offer to young children; the teaching of *tajwid*, that is, the proper pronunciation and intonation of the Holy Qur'an. But even in this area, they will have to learn the new techniques and technology of performing this job.

The main objective of teaching Islam to children should be to create a major positive change in their psycho-spiritual attitudes and give them general, comprehensible concepts about Islam; not simply to fill their heads with abstract, inert, religious material.

The Muslim educational psychologist should know, more than any other person, about the importance of example in the development of ethical values and religious attitudes; the importance of a model to be imitated and identified with; of a dynamic, popular teacher; a devoted, knowledgeable, warm person the kids love and respect; not an old sheikh nor a blind mullah.

In this comprehensive curriculum as much use as possible should be made of materials like films, television and other audio-visual aids the value of which research has proved, in the development of attitudes. Provision must be made for the expression of acquired ethical and spiritual appreciation through group dynamics, socialised class procedures, plays, field trips and camps.

If Muslim educational psychologists work very closely

with experts in curriculum development, methods, child development and rearing, as well as other interested educators to carry out this ambitious programme, then the courses of Islamic studies will be the most effective and popular in our schools. More importantly, we will be assured of having new generations of dynamic, devoted Muslim graduates who see much more in applied Islam than religious rites and the jurisdiction for marriage, divorce and inheritance.

Of course such research studies will require great expense which must be provided for by Muslim governments. Presidents and heads of Muslim states lose no chance of repeating the warm rhetoric of lip service to Islam as "the religion of the state" and "the true ideology of the nation". They should give a little concrete evidence of meaning what they say. Funds must be allocated to this vital project which may ultimately influence the whole future of Islam. Because of its importance, and the great similarity of its problems in various Muslim countries, it is advisable that this issue be approached as a pan-Islamic educational project subsidized by all interested Muslim states.

It is heartbreaking to know that communist governments are spending and doing much more in indoctrinating their young citizens and the world at large in atheistic Marxist philosophy than most Muslim states are doing for the cause of Islam.

iv. The Islamic social psychologist

Modern psychology can be put to the service of Islam in another important area. Muslim social psychologists, outside the lizard's hole, can carry out valuable studies delineating the psychosocial and spiritual factors underlying the great Islamic revolution which transformed the pre-Islamic ignorant crude bedouins to the most highly spiritualised and humanitarian society the world has ever known. For example, the wiping out of alcohol dependence and race segregation in the alcohol saturated and tribalistic pre-Islamic Arabia will be a subject of potential inspiration to young Muslim social scientists who study the great evils of alcoholism and colour bar in the modern "civilized" world.

One more example of a study of equal interest is research unearthing the sociocultural and spiritual factors underlying the unequalled military victories of Islam. In this connection, the Muslim social psychologist can explain ancient history in terms of newly developed sociocultural factors like the clarity and acceptability of war goals in Islamic jihad, brotherhood and *esprit de corps*, and the quality of Islamic leadership. Of course such studies must also serve to shed light on the causes of the contrasting, saddening condition of present day Islamic societies.

In fact, the most vital contribution of Muslim social psychologists is in this field of contemporary social and moral problems which beset all Muslim societies. One Muslim worker once said, "Islam is indeed the true revealed religion of God; otherwise how can so many people convert to Islam in spite of what they see in Muslim countries." In essence he is saying that Islam spreads in spite of the Muslims! This may seem to be an unjust statement. Though Muslim masses show many symptoms of decadence and other negative cultural qualities which are shared by the poor peoples of the so-called third world, they nevertheless possess many virtues and spiritual attributes extinguished in other nations by the strong influence of modern materialism. On the other hand, a critical unbiased investigation into the habits, practised morality, industriousness and general social life of Muslims in the light of the teachings of Islam will show a very vast gap indeed.

Many Muslim scholars have attributed this "credibility gap" to political, economic or general social factors. Some simply blame it on imperialism. To make a more rigorous study of this phenomenon, Muslim social psychologists have much to offer in collaboration with other social scientists and educators. We need to know, for example, more about the causes of decadence and indifference among our masses, and about the factors underlying the political tyranny and corruption in our government systems. How much of these, and similar ills, is really due to foreign imperialist influences? How much is due to our own weaknesses? What are these weaknesses and how can we outgrow them? What role should modern Muslim movements play in redressing this situation and why are such movements getting in trouble with their governments and peoples?

The whole future of work for Islam as a comprehensive way of life depends much on a strategy guided by such studies. Thus the Muslim social psychologist should appreciate the important role he can play and the services he can offer to Islam.

v. *An Islamic concept of personality*

Lastly I shall discuss some of the contributions of Muslim

personality theorists. As already mentioned, personality theory is a very challenging area of Western applied psychology, since it deals with issues of basic concern to religion and philosophy of life. Muslim personality theoreticians have many essential untapped issues to research in and theorise from. What were the personality theories of our ancient great Muslim scholars and philosophers like al-Ghazali, Ibn Rushd and Ibn Sina, and how do their theories compare with modern personality theory? What is the Islamic concept of human nature and how did this concept influence the early Muslims? How does it influence modern Muslims? How does it compare with the Judaeo-Christian concept of man and with the concepts upheld by modern Western personality theoreticians? What are the major biological, psychosocial and spiritual determinants, of personality stated in the Holy Qur'an, the hadith of Prophet Muhammad (ṣ) or by the early Muslim pioneers? Can these be weaved into a modern Islamic psychospiritual conceptualisation of personality?

As it appears, Muslim psychologists who specialise in the field of personality have thus far contributed very little in dealing with the above mentioned issues in a bold original manner.[54] A few even accept a Western personality theory with some conviction and then hypothesise about Islamic issues from its territory. This is like viewing a distant object by using a binocular the other way round.

It is true that personality theory can become a difficult

---

54. There are, of course, rare exceptions like the excellent paper, "Islamic perspectives of a balanced personality", presented by Dr. Rashid Hamid in the Fourth Annual Convention of the Association of Muslim Social Scientists in Indianapolis, USA in 1975.

and thorny subject when tackled purely from an Islamic point of view. For one thing we may not be able to strictly talk about an "Islamic theory of personality" in a precise manner. Islam to a Muslim is a revealed religion. It is the Truth. A psychological theory, on the other hand, is simply a set of conventions created by the theorist, in many ways, in an arbitrary creative manner, like an artist or a poet. As Hall and Lindsey[55] assert, theories are never true or false; they are only useful or not useful with respect to their efficiency in generating predictions or propositions which turn out to be verified.

Nevertheless the Holy Qur'an and the hadith explicitly speak of a number of specific explanatory concepts or causes for individual and collective behaviour of man. In the Holy Qur'an these causes are in fact considered psychospiritual and social natural laws, *Sunnah Allah*. A Muslim theoretician who is well grounded in Western academic psychology and in personality theory, and who is at the same time prepared to free himself from their negative influences, will be able to read into these social and psychospiritual Qur'anic natural laws a whole skeleton for an Islamic concept of personality. Flesh can later be built onto this skeleton from the Prophet's hadith and biography as well as from the works of early Muslim scholars. Thus, devout Muslim personality theoreticians may be able to offer the whole field of psychology a new dimension in personality theory.

It is worth noting in this connection that, already, eminent Western psychologists are beginning to appreciate

---

55. Hall and Lindsey, *op. cit.*

the contributions of other ancient non-Western, "psychologies" to modern personality theory. An important landmark in this respect is that Hall and Lindsey have included a chapter on "Eastern psychology" in the latest (1978) edition of their well known book *Theories of Personality*. In the opening paragraphs of this chapter they stated the following:

> Attempts to forge a systematic understanding of human personality and behaviour did not originate with contemporary Western psychology. Our formal psychology, about a hundred years old, is merely a recent version of an endeavour probably as old as human history. The theories of personality discussed in (this book) are the product of European and American culture, and only one set of innumerable 'psychologies' that people in many times and places have articulated. While the psychologies of some cultures and epochs have been at best loose collections of folk wisdom combined with imaginative myths, other peoples have developed theories of personality as sophisticated and as well grounded in empirical observations as our own.
>
> One of the richest sources of such well-formulated psychologies are Eastern religions".[56]

One sincerely hopes that this honest and open-minded attitude portrayed by these Western psychologists may encourage Muslim psychologists in deep lizard's holes to have another look at the psychology underlying their religious roots and their rich heritage, and not to be more

---

56. Hall and Lindsey, *op. cit.*, p. 347.

Western than such Western psychologists!

In this section, I have tried to give a brief statement about what a Muslim psychologist, outside the lizard's hole, can do in placing his professional training in the service of Islam.

CHAPTER 13

Are all schools of Western psychology soulless?

We have criticized the major schools of Western psychology, like behaviourism and psychoanalysis, in terms of their inability to appreciate and deal with deep Islamic psychospiritual phenomena. In one way or the other, these schools are greatly influenced by atheistic positivist philosophy, they may have a pessimistic or distorted concept of human nature, and are either too simplistic or too biased to explain and entertain religious and spiritual processes. This general criticism may give the wrong impression that all Western psychology is materialistic and "soulless"; that there are no Western psychological schools or leading psychologists who subscribe to a more positive attitude to the spiritual aspect of man and his religious values.

In fact, even some of Freud's early disciples strongly attacked him for his atheistic stand and for putting sex as the cornerstone of his libidinal theory. Some of them broke away and initiated their own rival schools. Prominent among these was Carl Jung. As early as 1914, Jung resigned his presidency of the newly formed International Psychoanalytic Society and later developed his new school of analytical psychology. His personality theory is much less deterministic than Freudian psychoanalysis and is more mystically and religiously oriented. He also laid much less emphasis on the role of human sex and aggression.

Muslim psychologists should read Jung for a broader perspective in dynamic psychology from a Judaeo-Christian religious view. However, they can benefit more from acquainting themselves with less mystical and more up-to-date schools with a simple positive attitude to religion and a clear efficacious applied system. Humanistic psychology is one such prominent modern school. It started to emerge as a major psychological movement in the 1950s and 1960s when Americans started to realize their spiritual emptiness in spite of their material affluence. As a broad movement, humanistic psychology has been much influenced by renowned psychologists such as Gordon Allport, Abraham Maslow and Carl Rogers.

Though humanistic psychology has been influenced by psychoanalysis and behaviourism, it is, nevertheless in significant disagreement with both. The great emphasis which behaviourists place on stimuli and observable behaviour is seen by humanistic psychologists as an over-simplification which neglects man's self and subjective inner experience, his complex behaviour like love, values and faith, as well as his potential for self direction and actualization. Thus humanistic psychology lay great emphasis on the self as a unifying theme which accounts for the individual's subjective experiences, and which determines much of his observable behaviour. In this respect, humanistic self-psychologists are much nearer to a religious psychophysical dualistic concept of man's body versus his soul or mind.

Humanistic psychologists also disagree with the pessimistic view of human nature portrayed by Freudian psychoanalysis as well as the neutral (neither evil nor good) view upheld by behaviourists. To them both schools wrongly see man's behaviour as fully determined by forces beyond his control; be it unconscious motives or early conditioning and environmental influences. In contrast, the humanistic model subscribes to a much more positive concept of human nature, viewing it as basically good. Selfish and cruel human acts are seen as pathological behaviour caused by the denial and frustration of this basic good nature. Man is not seen as a passive automaton, but as an active participant who has the freedom of choice to shape his destiny and that of his fellow men.

Muslim psychologists may compare these humanistic views with the Islamic concept of *fitra*, the inborn good nature given to man by his Creator, and the Islamic belief in man's responsibility for what he chooses to do in this life.

Another group of Western psychological theories, very much related to humanistic self-psychology, are those influenced by the existential model. In fact many humanistic psychologists are also referred to as existentialist in orientation. This is so because both schools emphasize the uniqueness of the individual, his quest for values, and his freedom for self-fulfilment. However, existentially oriented psychologists are less optimistic about modern man's ability to achieve self actualization in the dehumanizing contemporary western mass society. They also stress a few basic themes which should be of particular interest to the Muslim psychologist. Of these the theme of will to meaning, and that of existential anxiety and the encounter with nothingness are most pertinent.

These themes are very beautifully expounded by Viktor Frankl. He is one of the most outstanding existentially oriented psychiatrists whose works must be carefully read by all serious Muslim psychotherapists in spite of some of his religious biases. He founded his psychotherapeutic school of logotherapy out of his long bitter experiences in bestial Nazi concentration camps. "Logotherapy" comes from the Greek word logos which denotes "meaning" or "spirit". Thus logotherapy focuses on the meaning of man's existence and on his search for such a meaning.

To stimulate this search for meaning in them, Frank asks his desperate patients, ". . . since you find your life so miserable why do you not commit suicide?" From their answers, e.g. the love for a child, a mother or a spouse, dedication to a job or a party, Dr Frankl was able to bring together these driving forces which gave meaning to his patients' lives to the foreground of their psychic and spiritual existence. The motto of logotherapy is Niezche's famous statement, "he who has a why to live can bear with almost any how."[57] To him the main cause for the contemporary explosion of emotional disturbances is the frustration of modern man's will to meaning. Modern life has deprived man from seeing a real meaning or cause for which to live.

Will to meaning is then a basic human characteristic. Its

---

57. V. E. Frankl, *Man's Search for Meaning*, Hodder and Stoughton, London, 1964.

frustration leads to existential vacuum, to an encounter with nothingness; with non-being. This manifests itself mainly in a state of boredom and "existential anxiety" which may eventually lead to what Frankl calls a "noogenic neurosis". This is a neurosis which emerges as a result of moral and spiritual conflict between various values, rather than a conflict between drives and instincts as psychoanalysts believe.

This concept of existential vacuum and non-being should remind Muslim psychologists of the Qur'anic verses which describe the dilemma of life without faith in Allah as a state of 'spiritual non-being' in which the atheist loses touch with his own self! God, in Islam, is the only True Reality of which man is only a reflection. Hence to forget God is to alienate one's self from the very source of one's being. The Qur'an says:

> *And be not like those who forgot God and He caused them to forget their own selves or souls.*[58]

Also, the Muslim psychologist should find himself on familiar ground when reading about the theory proposed by Frankl and other existential analysts that modern life with its material wealth may actually increase the chances of agony and existential anxiety for the modern man. Islam considers the spiritual meaning derived from submission to God as the only true meaning for man in this life. Furthermore, the Qur'an speaks of material wealth as a form of punishment to those who live in a "spiritual vacuum".

---

58. Qur'an, 59: 19.

> *Do not be dazzled by their wealth nor their (following in) sons. God's plan is to punish them with these (material) things in this life before their souls perish in disbelief and denial of God.*[59]

As is expected, religion is highly placed in Frankl's logotherapy since, as he says, it is the greatest force which gives meaning to man's continued sufferings. Listen to what he has to say about the role of religion in concentration camps:

> The religious interest of prisoners, as far and as soon as it developed, was the most sincere imaginable. The depth and vigor of religious belief often surprised and moved a new arrival. Most impressive in this connection were improvised prayers and services in the corner of a hut, or in the darkness of the locked cattle truck in which we were brought back from a distant work site, tired, hungry and frozen in our ragged clothing.[60]

Thus, in comparison to Freud, Frankl takes this contrasting attitude to religion. He bitterly criticises psychoanalytically oriented theoreticians who explain all sorts of human activities, even the most humane and noble of them, in terms of base unconscious motives and defence mechanisms. The following short quotation serves well to illustrate this:

> Man's search for meaning is a primary force in his life

---

59. Qur'an, 9: 55.

60. Frankl, *op. cit.*, p. 33.

and not a 'secondary rationalization' of instinctual drives. This meaning is unique and specific in that it must and can be fulfilled by him alone; only then does it achieve a significance which will satisfy his own will to meaning. There are some authors who contend that meanings and values are nothing but defence mechanisms, reaction formations and sublimations. But as for myself, I would not be willing to live merely for the sake of my 'defence mechanisms', nor would I be ready to die for the sake of my 'reaction formations'. Man, however, is able to live and even die for the sake of his ideals and values![61]

If such a psychiatrist is able to see the importance of religious ideals and values in the materialistic Western society and its degenerating Jewish and Christian religions, and is able to initiate a successful school of psychotherapy on its foundation, what excuse have the Muslim psychologists who continue to parrot the atheistic views of Freud and other psychologists in their comparatively religious and moralistic societies.

---

61. Frankl, *ibid.*, p. 99.

CHAPTER 14

What about soulless schools of Western psychology?

So far I have been discussing some of the useful areas in modern psychology which Islamists can adapt and accept, but what about those areas like psychoanalysis which have hostile attitudes to religion and a distorted concept of man. Shall we throw such material out of our Muslim university curricula as some Muslim educators demand? The reader may be surprised by a negative answer to this question. Islamic countries cannot isolate themselves from modern Western civilization and its harmful impact, but we can "vaccinate" our Muslim students against the harmful "infections" of Westernisation. If, for example, we do not teach psychoanalysis, they will see films which sensationally portray the ugly aspects of the theory as scientific facts; they will hear it over the radio and read it in short stories in magazines. Thus such a theory must be critically taught in order to be severely stripped from the Islamic and scientific points of view. Alternative neutral or Islamic theory should then be introduced. But in spite of their irreligious stand, an effort must be made to do justice to these theories, showing what is true and what is false in them. The true aspects, as Eysenck said, will not be new and the Islamic psychologist will almost certainly find their roots in Islam and the contributions of early and modern Islamic thinkers.

Take Freud's theories on child development. The material on infantile sexuality as portrayed by such postulates as the Oedipus complex is new, and its falsification has already been stated. The importance of love, warmth and a permissive attitude to children and their relation to healthy development is true. Though this might have been a great discovery for Westerners, it was not so for Muslims. Our Qur'an, our ḥadith, the life of our Prophet Muhammad (ṣ), and his history is full of direct and implied teachings on being warm and kind to children and treating them as children, not miniature adults. Such behaviour, as exemplified by the Prophet (ṣ), reflect the true essence of permissiveness. The love of the Prophet (ṣ) for children and his permissive attitude to them is unequalled. He once lengthened the time of his prostration in prayer until his companions felt tired. When they enquired after the prayer was finished, he told them that his grandchild had ridden on his blessed back while he was prostrating himself and that he had not wished to rise before the child finished his play.

He also used to carry his female baby grandchild during his prayer at a time in which the Arabs used to bury their female daughters alive for economic and moral reasons! Not only does the Qur'an attack this custom but it also severely shuns the very segregation between male and female children:

> *When news is brought to one of them, of the (birth of) a female (child), his face darkens, and he is filled with grief!*
>
> *With shame does he hide himself from his people, because of the bad news he has had! Shall he keep it (the child) in contempt or bury it in the dust? Verily evil is their judgement.*[62]

Such references will give an Islamic dimension to modern theory and refer their true components to their true origin.

Sex is another area of interest in this connection. The exaggerated place of sex in Freudian theory, which claims that almost all human activities are consciously or unconsciously motivated by sex is false. The outmoded psychoanalytic contention that all neuroses are caused by sexual repressions and unresolved Oedipal conflicts is also false. It was partly an overreaction to the Catholic and or Victorian repressive ethics which prevailed in Freud's time. Whereas the fact that children should not be misinformed or punished when they ask questions pertaining to sex and that they should be given pertinent suitable sexual information which they can comprehend and which helps them to treat sex as a natural biological phenomenon is true. This approach will make them grow as adults who do not associate sex with undue, exaggerated, feelings of shame, guilt and sinfulness. Though these facts were only recently established in the West as a result of Freudian influences, they are definitely not new to Muslims. The

---

62. Qur'an, 16: 58-59.

Qur'an, which is the greatest source of spiritual guidance, is also a guide in matters pertaining to sex education. It tells us and tells our children in simple poetic language which they can understand, about the development of human life inside the mother's womb. It refers to sex as a gift from Allah to mankind and that its joys will be bestowed on the faithful in Paradise. It even shows the falsity of Jewish myths about the alleged dangers that may happen to a baby if the mother becomes pregnant while she is taking a particular position during sexual intercourse. In this subject, the Qur'an speaks about sexual intercourse in terms of "cultivation", and refutes the conviction, strongly believed in at the time by the Jews and the Arabs of Medina, that the time or position taken during intercourse physically affects the development of the baby to be born:

> *Your wives are as tilth or cultivation for you; so approach your tilth when or how you please.*[63]

Since all this information comes to us from the Qur'an and from the hadith of our Prophet (ṣ) there will be no undue shame and guilt with regard to sex practised within the limits of Islamic morality. 'Aishah, the Prophet's wife, says: "Truly wonderful are the women of the Ansar. Shame about sex has not prevented them from learning their religious commands."[64]

Thus, with regard to sex, we as practising Muslims should not have the extreme Catholic feelings of guilt and sinfulness which are considered as the main cause of

---

63. Qur'an, 2: 223.

64. al-Bukhari, *Bab al-'Ilm*.

impotence and frigidity in the West.[65] We do not need to be introduced to such Freudian principles by the modern sex educators.

If we see in the Muslim world of today many harsh, traditional fathers who do not show affection and warmth to their children, and if we find a few modern Muslims bearing a Catholic attitude towards sex, then it is not because of Islam, it is because of failure to follow its teachings.

So, in this section, we have tried to show that Muslim psychologists who critically probe 'soulless' schools of Western psychology, can find some useful aspects in them, and can even trace some of these good aspects to Islamic sources.

---

65. Masters and Johnson as quoted by Bellivaeau, *Understanding Human Sexual Inadequacy*, Coronet Books, London, 1974.

CHAPTER 15

How to help them out of the Pit?

I shall now come to the last item in this study. That is my answer to the question, "what can the Islamic psychologist do about his colleagues who enter the lizard's hole?"

According to my short experience in this field, I believe that the "psychology" of such Muslim psychologists can be divided into three distinct phases in the process of getting into and out of the lizard's hole; these are the infatuation, reconciliation, and liberation phases.

i. The phase of infatuation

Young Muslims in training are generally thrilled by psychology and its clever techniques. They are open to suggestion and generally take their instructor's ideas and what they read as facts which they are anxious to apply on actual behaviour. Their acquaintances believe that they have become experts at knowing what goes on in human minds and how to "analyse" people. Many of them are flattered and happy about this acquired prestige. They gradually slip into lizard's holes because this gives them security and pride. If they are practising Muslims at this phase they tend to develop the dual personality systems of mental and emotional compartmentalisation which I have already mentioned; *i.e.*, that of a Freudian and practising Muslim living harmoniously in the same body and psychic system.

ii. The phase of reconciliation

However, as time goes by, and they discover with postgraduate studies what psychology can really do and what it cannot, and as they begin to feel their way back to a more dynamic Muslim scholar, they try to bridge the gap of cognitive dissonance by an artificial compromise between Islam and psychological theory. They may state happily that there is no serious conflict between Islam and Jungian theory, or that the Qur'an gives support to Freudian theory on the structure of personality of which the components are the "id", the "ego" and the "superego". To prove their point they may quote verses from the Holy Qur'an that speak about *al-Nafs* (self or soul), a*l-Nafs al-Ammara* (the self or soul that orders one to do evil things), and a*l-Nafs al-Lawama* (the accusing self or soul). Sometimes they may twist the meaning of Qur'anic verses or hadith, or at least look for a far-fetched meaning in order to ease their frustration of dissonance.

iii. The phase of emancipation

The third and last phase is the one in which they come to realise that though modern schools of psychology and Islam may have a number of aspects in which they exhibit some superficial similarities, they are essentially totally different phenomena which have different concepts about life, about the place of man in this universe and about his destiny. They will come to realise that they are first and foremost Muslims and then psychologists. That their jobs and limited knowledge should serve their faith and ideology, not the other way around. That they should be honest with themselves and with the people who seek their services in telling them what they can really do and what they cannot. That they must overcome the temptation to keep the false halo effect of all knowing "experts" of the human mind and modestly use their new positions in the genuine help of Muslims. They can do a lot in clearing their misinterpretations about Islam and giving them greater confidence in themselves and in their Creator, Allah, the Most High.

Muslim psychologists can develop from phase one to phase three if they possess the minimum Islamic impetus and if they find the right type of experiences. If they do not, what can the liberated Islamic psychologist do about his brothers in phases one and two?

I believe that he should devote much of his efforts to the young enthusiastic psychologists to prevent their gradual decline into the lizard's hole. He must do his best to uncover the weaknesses of the un-Islamic aspects of psychology and to support his arguments by current research before seeking the support of pure Islamic evidence. He can then tell them about the merits of alternative psychological schools of thought which do not have similar contradiction with Islamic ideology.

If such an Islamic psychologist is a university professor he will have to shoulder a greater responsibility in this respect. However, he may incite much resistance and enmity from his colleagues who dogmatically follow and support certain schools of psychology and who have themselves secured their positions in the lizard's hole. Many of these professors will feel naked and ignorant outside their holes and so they will not like colleagues who disturb their comfort.

Many modern Muslim thinkers do not have patience with those who make artificial compromises between Islam and the theories of the physical sciences, let alone the culture-bound Western theories of the social sciences. However, the emancipated Islamic psychologist should be lenient and kind to the one who is in stage two; that of compromising between psychology and Islam. Such a person is in a state of conflict and as I have said, is trying hard to bridge the gap of cognitive dissonance between his faith and his professional interests. He is half way out of the lizard's hole and one should encourage him to feel more secure outside of it. A harsh verbal attack by an enthusiastic Islamic psychologist on his ideas may make him act like a real lizard and rush back into his hole. He might have thought that his ideas were original and that they served Islam by portraying it as a modern ideology. Hence he expected his ideas to be warmly accepted by an Islamic colleague. The rebuff might render him antagonistic to Islamists altogether, and lead him to refuse to come out of his hole again. He might continue to give lip service to Islam, in relation to non-Islamic Western psychological theory, while in the presence of enthusiastic Islamic psychologists but his real existence would continue to be in his lizard's hole. He becomes like a real lizard which, when chased and sensing real danger to its life, breaks off its tail and rushes into its hole. Though he is in the safe darkness of his pit, his tail will continue to wiggle on the outside to cheat the aggressive chaser.

Of course an active Islamic psychological society with frequent scholarly meetings in which papers are read, published and circulated and in which Islamic psychologists can cooperate in publishing a journal of Islamic psychology can be of unlimited help in changing passive Muslim psychologists into dynamic practising Islamic scholars.

However, a group of older psychologists will continue to resist leaving their holes. They have stayed in there for too long and have acquired high status by so doing. Some of them love themselves more, or love Islam less, and hence will continue propagating Freudian fiction as scientific fact. They have grown too fat to leave their unclean shelters. One cannot but leave such persons to die in their dusty holes, the unblessed graves they have chosen for themselves.

> "Nor are the living equal with the dead. Allah makes whom he will to hear. You can't reach those who are in the graves".[66]

---

66. Qur'an, 35: 22.

References

al-Qur'an

Hadith of al-Bukhari and al-Muslim.

Allport, G., *The Individual and his Religion*, Macmillan, New York, 1953.

Al-Haj, F., *Al-Ghazali's concept of the conditioned reflex*, unpublished Ph.D. thesis.

Anastasi, A., *Psychological Testing*, Macmillan, New York, 1968.

Badri, M. B., A new technique for the systematic desensitisation of pervasive anxiety and phobic reactions, *Journal of Psych.*, 65, 201-208.

Badri, M. B., Culture, traditions and psychopathology, *Sudan Medical Journal*, 10, 1972.

Badri, M. B., *The Psychology of Children's Drawings* (in Arabic), Al-Fath Publications, Beirut, 1966.

Badri, M. and Dennis, D., Human-figure drawings in

relation to modernisation in Sudan, *Journal of Psych.*, 58, 1964.

Bakan, D., *On Methods*, Jessey Inc., San Francisco, 1969.

Bakan, D., *Sigmund Freud and the Jewish Mystical Tradition*, Van Nostrand Co., Princeton, 1958.

Bellivaeau, F. and Richter, L., *Understanding Human Sexual Inadequacy*, Cornet Books, London, 1974.

Coleman, J., *Abnormal Psychology and Modern Life*, Scott Foresman, 1961.

Ellenberger, H. F., *The Discovery of the Unconscious*, Allen Lane, The Penguin Press, London, 1970.

Ellis, A., *Sex Without Guilt*, Wilshire Book Co., Hollywood, Calif., 1974.

Eysenck, H. J., Experimental study of Freudian concepts, *Bulletin of the Brit. Psych. Society*, 25, 89, 1972.

Fink, P., and Hammett, V., *Sexual Function and Dysfunction*, Davis Co., Philadelphia, 1969.

Frankl, V. E., *Man's Search for Meaning*, Hodder and Stoughton, London, 1964.

Frankl, V., *Psychotherapy and Existentialism*, Clarion Book Co., 1967.

Freud, S., *Obsessive acts and religious practices.*

Freud, S., *New Introductory Lectures on Psychoanalysis*, Pelican Books, 1973.

Gilder, G., *Sexual Suicide*, Bantam Book, New York, 1975.

Hall, C. S., and Lindsey G., *Theories of Personality*, Wiley,

New York, 1978.

Jehoda, M., Social psychology and psychoanalysis: a mutual challenge, *Bulletin of the British Psych. Soc.*, 25, 89, 1972.

Malinowski, B., *Sex and Repression in Savage Society*, Harcourt, Brace & Co., New York, 1927.

Milleegi, A., *Religious Development in Children and Adolescents* (in Arabic), Dar al-Ma'arif, Cairo, 1955.

Prothro, E. T., *Child Rearing in the Lebanon*, Harvard Middle Eastern Monograph Series, 1961.

Rachman, R. S., *The Effects of Psychotherapy*, Pergamon Press, 1971.

Robert, M., *From Oedipus to Moses*, Routledge and Kegan Paul, London, 1977.

Skinner, B. F., *Beyond Freedom and Dignity*, Bantam Books, New York, 1975.

Stafford-Clark, D., *What Freud Really Said*, Pelican Books, 1969.

Storr, A., *The Integrity of Personality*, Pelican Books, 1974.

Szasz, T. S., *The Myth of Mental Illness*, Harper and Row, New York, 1974.

Index

Prepared by Dr A.S. Thorley.

A

Abnormality, psychological, 14–22, 28
Alcoholism, 84-86
Allah, 9, 32, 54, 55, 63, 71, 72, 95, 101, 105, 107
   Western psychology and Muslim emancipation, 95, 101, 104-107
Allport, G., 73, 74, 92
al-Nafs, 104
al-Nafs al-Ammara, 104
al-Nafs al-Lawaama, 104
anal character, 49-50, 58
Anastasi, A., 36
anti-psychiatry, 16
Arab (—ic), 9-10, 17, 37, 40-41, 54-55, 99-101
   proverb 37
Aristotle, 66
Association of Muslim Social Scientists (A.M.S.S.), 1, 87

B

Badri, M. and Dennis, W., 40,
Bakan, D., 48, 60
Bedouins, Arab, 9-10, 41, 85
behaviourism, behaviour-therapy, 2-13, 63, 68, 71-72, 74, 91-92

C

Cathexis, 57
Catholicism, 12, 100-102
chivalry, 18
Christianity, 2, 97 *see also* Judaeo-Christianity
clinical cases, 51, 71-77
co-education, 42-45
Coleman, J., 29
Communism, 84
complexes, 36, 42, 50 *see also* Oedipus complex *and* penis envy
compulsive stealing, 19
conditioned reflexes, 7-11
counselling, non-directive, 76
credibility gap between Islam and Western psychology, 86

D

Delinquency, 29
Dennis, Wayne, 40
desensitisation, 71, 74, 76
draw-a-person-test, 40
drugs, 71, 74, 75

E

Educational psychology, 42-47, 68, 80-84
ego defense mechanisms, 50-54, 97
electro-convulsive theraphy (E.C.T.), 74
electro-sleep therapy, 74
Ellenberger, H.F., 23-24, 55, 59
emancipation of Muslim, 120-107
erogenous oral zone, 57
existentialism, 104-107
experimental psychology, 14, 68
Eysenck, H.J., 60, 99

F

fahisha, 71
family systems, 28-32
feminism, 44
fitra, 56, 93
Frankl, Victor, 58, 94- 97
Freud, Sigmund, 23, 24, 25, 35, 48, 49, 50, 53, 54, 55, 56, 57, 58, 59, 60, 61, 62, 63, 91, 96, 97, 99, 100
  Muslim emancipation, 104-105, 107

G

al-Ghazali, 10, 66, 87
God, attitudes towards:
  Behaviourist, 5, 7, 9-10

Index

Frankl's, 58
Freud's, 21, 24, 53-55
Islamic, 55-56, 58, 85, 95-96

H

Habib, Dr H., 72
Hadith, 1-2, 81, 86-89, 99, 101, 104
al-Haj, Dr Faiz, 10
Halal or Haram, 6
Hall, C.S. and Lindsay, G., 11
Hamid, Dr Rasheed, 77, 87
Hedonism, 7, 11-12
"here and now", 5
homosexuality, 19, 45
House-Tree-Person (H.T.P), 35, 37, 40
Humanistic psychology, 92-93
hypnotism, 55

I

Ibn Khaldun, 66
Ibn Rushd, 87
Ibn Sina, 66, 87
Ibn Sirin, 66
Id, 49, 57, 104
Imam, 74-75
infatuation with psychology, 103-104
Institute Ar-Rashad, 1

International Psychoanalytical Society, 92
Islam(—ic) attitudes towards:
Behaviourism, 11-12;
children, 28-33;
Freud and psychoanalysis, 48-51, 55-56;
Ideology, 23-26;
Muslim emanciaption, 104-107;
Western psychology, 65-67, 70-90, 112-117

J

jihad, 85
Jiha's water wheel, 37
Judaeo-Christianity, 2, 11, 87, 92
Judaism, 2, 60-61, 97, 100-101
Jung, Carl, 92, 104

K

Kafir psychology, 66, 69
Khalil, M.Y, 78
Khartoum, clinic, 75
al-Kousi, Abdul Azeez, 67

L

Learning theory and aids, 67-68, 95-96
libido, 49, 57

Lindsay, G., 88

Lizard's Holes, 1-2, 12-14, 26-32, 37, 42, 47
psychoanalysis, 47-48, 52, 60-61, 63
Islamic psychology, 65, 70, 78, 85, 89, 103-107

logos, 94

logotherapy, 94, 96

Lot, 19, 20

M

Machover's draw-a-person test, 40

Malinowski, 58

Maslow, A.H., 92

masochism, 19

mass media, 2

mental illness, 16 *see also* clinical cases

Milleegi, Dr. A., 52

Mittleman, 20

Muhammad, Prophet, 32, 61, 76, 99

al-Muhasibi, 66

Moses, 60-61

Muslim psychologists, 66, 77

N

Nazi concentration camps, 94

Niezche, F., 94

"Noogenic neurosis", 95

O

Obsesssional neurosis and symptoms, 24-25, 53, 69, 71-75

Oedipus complex, 38, 48-51, 63-55, 58, 60-61, 63; judgements, 99-101

P

Parental permissiveness, 28-33

Pavlov, I.P.,, 9

"penis envy", 37-38, 54

personality, 2, 14, 20, 25, 27, 34, 36, 66, 73, 86, 87, 88, 89, 92, 104

philosophy, 6, 14, 23, 45, 48, 62, 68, 84, 87, 91

positivism, 24, 91

projection, projective test, 35-38

prophets, *see* Lot, Muhammad, Shu'ayb

psychoanalysis, 3, 25, 26, 48, 49, 52, 53, 57, 58, 59, 60, 61, 62, 91, 92, 93, 98

psychological tests, value of, 34, 78

Index

psychology *see* educational humanistic social and Western

psychometry, 34-41, 78-80

psychospiritual, concepts, 7, 12, 77, 87, 88, 91

psychotherapy, 63, 66, 67, 68, 70, 71, 76, 97

Q

Qur'an, 9, 19-21, 32
  psychology, 81-83, 87-88, 95-96, 99-101, 104-105
  psychotherapy, 72, 75

Qutb, Mohammed, 65

R

Rachmann, R.S., 63

Ramadhan, month of, 75

ar-Rashad, Institute, 1

rationalization, secondary, 97

reconciliation of Islam and Western psychology, 104

re-inforcement of learning, 4, 9, 11

religion, Freud, 10-12, 23, 25, 52-53, 62;
  Islam, 82-88, 91, 96-97

"repression", 38, 42, 50

revolutionary groups, 79

Rogers, Carl, 92

Rorschach Test, 35, 37-38

S

Sadism, 17

Saudi Arabia, 1, 10, 66

senility, 45

sex-education, 42-44, 83, 100-101

Sherif, 67

Shu'ayb, 19

Skinner, B.F., 6, 7, 9

social psychology, 66-70

Stafford-Clark, D.,, 25

statistics, 16, 63

Stimulus-Response, 11

style of life, Islamic, 82

subjectivity, 36

Sudanese custom of flogging volunteers during marriage ceremonies, 17-20

Suef, Mustafa, 67

Sunnah Allah, 88

superego, 104

Swellin, Atttya, 77

Szasz, T.S., 16

T

Tajwid, 83

Talmund, 60
Tarawih prayers, 75
Trade, 55-56
Thematic Apperception Test (T.A.T), 35, 37-38, 41
transcendentalism, 20, 73
Trobriand islanders, 58

U

"Unconcious", 53, 59, 96
Universities: al-Azhar, Cairo, 82
  Jordan, 41
  Khartoum, Sudan, 37
  Mohammed Ibn Saud, Saudi Arbia, 10
  Muslim, 64, 66, 82

Omdurman, Sudan, 82
Riyadh, Saudi Arabia, 1

V

"Verbalism", 82

W

Watson, H.B., 9
Western psychology, 21, 25-26, 34, 43-44, 46-47, 57, 63
  Muslim views, 65-69, 86-88, 91-102
wudu', 75

Z

Zewar Prof. M, 52-55, 63

Made in the USA
Las Vegas, NV
12 May 2022